END TIMES PROPHECY

END TIMES PROPHECY

Ancient Wisdom for Uncertain Times

JOHN F. WALVOORD

David C Cook®
transforming lives together

END TIMES PROPHECY
Published by David C Cook
4050 Lee Vance View
Colorado Springs, CO 80918 U.S.A.

David C Cook Distribution Canada
55 Woodslee Avenue, Paris, Ontario, Canada N3L 3E5

David C Cook U.K., Kingsway Communications
Eastbourne, East Sussex BN23 6NT, England

The graphic circle C logo is a registered trademark of David C Cook.

LCCN 2015960922
ISBN 978-1-4347-0991-2
eISBN 978-0-7814-1432-6

The Team: Tim Peterson, Keith Wall, Amy Konyndyk,
Nick Lee, Jack Campbell, Susan Murdock
Cover Design: Jon Middel
Cover Photo: Thinkstock

Printed in the United States of America
First Edition 2016

1 2 3 4 5 6 7 8 9 10

012816

CONTENTS

REPLACING CONFUSION WITH CLARITY AND ANXIETY WITH ASSURANCE

Mention the words *end times* and most people will respond with a combination of fascination and fear, confusion and conjecture. No doubt the Bible's scores of prophecies about the rapture, tribulation, and other world-shaking occurrences fuel our imagination and grip our hearts.

End times events have been the source of many popular fiction series, movies, and theatrical productions. The storylines of these dramatizations are, of course, intended to entertain and enthrall, not accurately educate individuals. So these depictions often leave readers and viewers with a distorted image of the rapture and subsequent events. What is more, sermons, books, and articles by well-meaning teachers and authors often leave people more perplexed than precise in their understanding. It's no wonder so many are confused—and frightened—about the end times.

The Bible is full of references to the future—a future that will see one era of human history end and a vastly different one begin. For those interested in studying these issues, the challenge is that prophecy is often presented as a conglomeration of differing views, various interpretations of Scripture, baffling charts and timelines, and puzzling terminology.

The book you hold in your hands is intended to clear up much of the confusion and, in many ways, relieve fears for those who have placed their trust in God's Son, Jesus Christ. It's true that words such as *Antichrist* and *Armageddon* evoke images that frighten us. It's also true that God's Word promises that the Creator of the universe, our heavenly Father, loves His children deeply and promises a future full of unimaginably good things.

The approach taken in the pages that follow is straightforward: As much as possible, we will allow Scripture to speak for itself on matters of prophecy. We will let God's Word reveal His intent and plan for the end times. We have included commentary on many passages simply to provide context and to clarify terms and references that might be unfamiliar to modern readers. Prophecies have been organized and grouped according to themes for easy navigation through this material. It is our prayer that this book will serve as an open door for God to speak to your heart and mind regarding your place in future events. Most of all, may you draw courage and comfort in knowing that the God who created everything is still, and will always be, firmly in control.

UNDERSTANDING PROPHECY IN CONTEXT

In the history of the church, the prophetic portions of Scripture have suffered more from inadequate interpretation than any other major theological subject. The reason is that the church turned aside from a normal and literal interpretation of prophecy to one that is nonliteral and subject to the whims of the interpreter. This false approach to interpreting prophecy is contradicted by the fact that many hundreds of prophecies have already been literally fulfilled.

In the first two centuries of the Christian era, the church was predominantly "premillennial," interpreting Scripture to teach that Christ would fulfill the prophecy of His second coming to bring a thousand-year reign on earth before the eternal state began. This was considered normal in orthodox theology. The early interpretation of prophecy was not always cogent and sometimes fanciful, but for the most part, prophecy was treated the same way as other scripture.

At the end of the second century and through the third century, the heretical school of theology at Alexandria, Egypt, advanced the erroneous principle that the Bible should be interpreted in a nonliteral or allegorical sense. In applying this principle to the Scriptures, they subverted all the major doctrines of the faith, including prophecy. The early church emphatically denied the Alexandrian system and to a large extent restored the interpretation of Scripture to its literal, grammatical, historical sense. The problem was that in prophecy there were predictions that had not yet been fulfilled. This made it more difficult to prove that literal fulfillment was true of prophecy. The result was somewhat catastrophic for the idea of a literal interpretation of prophecy, and the church floundered in the area of interpreting future events.

Augustine (AD 354–430) rescued the church from uncertainty as far as nonprophetic Scripture was concerned, but he continued to treat prophecy in a nonliteral way with the purpose of eliminating a millennial kingdom on earth. Strangely, Augustine held to a literal second coming, a literal heaven, and a literal hell, but not to a literal millennium. This arbitrary distinction has never been explained.

Because "amillennialism" (which denies a literal millennial kingdom on earth following the second coming) is essentially negative and hinders literal interpretation of prophecy, there was little progress in this area. The church continued to believe in heaven and hell and purgatory but neglected or dismissed Old Testament passages dealing with Israel in prophecy and the kingdom on earth. Even in the Protestant Reformation, prophecy was not rescued from this hindrance in its interpretation.

Though remnants of the church still advanced the premillennial view, it was not until the nineteenth and twentieth centuries that a serious movement began to restore the literal truth of prophecy. The twentieth century was especially significant in the progress of prophetic interpretation in that many details of prophecy were debated and clarified in a way not previously done.

The importance of prophecy should be evident, even superficially, in examining the Christian faith, since about one-fourth of the Bible was written as prophecy. It is evident that God intended to draw aside the veil of the future and to give some indication of what His plans and purposes were for the human race and for the universe as a whole. The neglect and misinterpretation of Scriptures supporting the premillennial interpretation are now to some extent being corrected.

For Christians, a solid hope for the future is essential. Christianity without a future would not be basic Christianity. In contrast to the beliefs of some other religions, which often paint the future in a forbidding way, Christianity's hope is bright and clear, assuring the Christian that the life to come will be better than the present one. As Paul stated in 2 Corinthians 5:8, "We are confident, I say, and would prefer to be away from the body and at home with the Lord." In the Christian faith, the future is painted as one of bliss and happiness in the presence of the Lord without the ills that are common to this life.

The revelation of prophecy in the Bible serves as important evidence that the Scriptures are accurate in their interpretation of the future. Because approximately half of the prophecies of the Bible have already been fulfilled in a literal way, we have a strong intellectual basis for assuming that prophecy yet to be fulfilled will likewise have a literal fulfillment. At the same time, we can rightly conclude that the Bible is inspired of the Holy Spirit and that prophecy is indeed a revelation by God for that which is certain to come.

Scriptural prophecy, properly interpreted, also provides a guideline for establishing the value of human conduct and the things that pertain to this life. For Christians, the ultimate question is whether

God considers what we are doing of value, in contrast to the world's system of values, which is largely materialistic.

Prophecy also provides a guide to the meaning of history. Though philosophers will continue to debate a philosophy of history, the Bible indicates that history is the unfolding of God's plan and purpose for revealing Himself and manifesting His love. In the Christian faith, history reaches its climax in God's plan for the future in which the earth in its present situation will be destroyed and a new earth will be created. A proper interpretation of prophecy serves to support and enhance all other areas of theology, and without a proper interpretation of prophecy, all other areas to some extent become incomplete revelation.

In attempting to accurately communicate the meaning of Scripture, prophecy serves to bring light and understanding to many aspects of our present life as well as our future hope. In an effort to understand and interpret prophecy correctly as a justifiable theological exercise, it is necessary to establish a proper base for interpretation.

1

AN END TIMES TIMELINE

Because there is so much confusion and disagreement about the end times, even among Christians, this chapter is meant to serve as an overview—a timeline that will help you visualize the major events of unfulfilled prophecy. In this chapter, you will see summaries of occurrences from the rapture through Christ's final judgment and the beginning of the eternal heavenly reign. Each of these events will be dealt with at more length throughout the rest of the book.

1. Rapture of the Church (1 Cor. 15:51–58; 1 Thess. 4:13–18)

The first concrete event of the end times is the rapture, the moment when Jesus Christ takes up all believers to be with Him in heaven, before the turmoil and persecution of the tribulation begins.

> Brothers and sisters, we do not want you to be uninformed about those who sleep in death, so that you do not grieve like the rest of mankind, who have no hope.… For the Lord himself will come down from heaven, with a loud command, with the voice of the archangel and with the trumpet call of

God, and the dead in Christ will rise first. After
that, we who are still alive and are left will be caught
up together with them in the clouds to meet the
Lord in the air. And so we will be with the Lord
forever. (1 Thess. 4:13, 16–17)

This revelation was introduced as truth that is "according to
the Lord's word" (v. 15), given to the apostle Paul by special revelation. Though Jesus introduced the doctrine of the rapture in John
14:1–3, there was no exposition of it while He was still on earth.
This revelation, given to Paul to pass on to the Thessalonian church,
becomes an important additional message concerning the nature of
the rapture.

2. Revival of the Roman Empire; Ten-Nation Confederacy Formed (Dan. 7:7, 24; Rev. 13:1; 17:3, 12–13)

Specific political realities have also been predicted in Scripture.
Alliances and wars will happen according to prophecy.

After that, in my vision at night I looked, and there
before me was a fourth beast—terrifying and fright-
ening and very powerful. It had large iron teeth;
it crushed and devoured its victims and trampled
underfoot whatever was left. It was different from
all the former beasts, and it had ten horns.…

The ten horns are ten kings who will come
from this kingdom. After them another king will
arise, different from the earlier ones. (Dan. 7:7, 24)

In Daniel's vision, the four beasts represented four kingdoms. The fourth kingdom was not named but was historically fulfilled by the Roman Empire. As described in verse 7, it crushed and devoured the countries it conquered. The ten horns represented a future Roman Empire that will reappear in the end times.

3. Rise of the Antichrist: The Middle East Dictator (Dan. 7:8; Rev. 13:1–8)

The leader of this new Roman Empire is also predicted. Daniel's beastly metaphor continues:

> There before me was another horn, a little one, which came up among them; and three of the first horns were uprooted before it. This horn had eyes like the eyes of a human being and a mouth that spoke boastfully. (Dan. 7:8)

The Antichrist will be known by his boastful arrogance and for setting himself up against God's authority.

4. The Seven-Year Peace Treaty with Israel: Consummated Seven Years before the Second Coming of Christ (Dan. 9:27; Rev. 19:11–16)

This Antichrist will deal duplicitously with God's chosen nation, Israel.

> He will confirm a covenant with many for one "seven."
> In the middle of the "seven" he will put an end to sac-
> rifice and offering. And at the temple he will set up an

> abomination that causes desolation, until the end that
> is decreed is poured out on him. (Dan. 9:27)

This treaty will initially be seen as a positive mark of this world ruler's leadership. The leader will be charismatic and popular, hence his worldwide sway and influence.

5. Establishment of a World Church (Rev. 17:1–15)

The significant events won't be marked only by secular politics. There will be effects in the religious sphere as well.

> One of the seven angels who had the seven bowls came and said to me, "Come, I will show you the punishment of the great prostitute, who sits by many waters." …
> The name written on her forehead was a mystery: Babylon the Great, the Mother of Prostitutes and of the Abominations of the Earth. (Rev. 17:1, 5)

Since true believers have already been raptured, those left on earth merely professed faith in Jesus but were not truly part of the church invisible. Those who remain—whatever they claim—will be part of the remnants of a universal "Babylonian" church. This church will dominate the world politically and religiously up to the midpoint of the last seven years before Christ's second coming.

6. Russia Springs a Surprise Attack on Israel Four Years before the Second Coming of Christ (Ezek. 38–39)

While the entire tribulation is marked by "wars and rumors of wars," things will now get specific.

> Son of man, set your face against Gog, of the land of Magog, the chief prince of Meshek and Tubal [or Rosh]....
>
> Get ready; be prepared, you and all the hordes gathered about you, and take command of them. After many days you will be called to arms. In future years you will invade a land that has recovered from war, whose people were gathered from many nations to the mountains of Israel, which had long been desolate. They had been brought out from the nations, and now all of them live in safety. (Ezek. 38:2, 7–8)

The ancient princes listed in Ezekiel 38 correspond with modern-day Russia. But there will be an alliance of several groups and nations that suddenly wage war against Israel.

7. Peace Treaty with Israel Broken after Three and a Half Years: Beginning of World Government, World Economic System, World Atheistic Religion, Final Three and a Half Years before the Second Coming of Christ (Dan. 7:23; Rev. 13:5–8, 15–17; 17:16–17)
The Antichrist's predicted and inevitable betrayal of Israel will occur halfway through the seven-year tribulation.

> [The beast] was given power to wage war against God's holy people and to conquer them. And it was

> given authority over every tribe, people, language
> and nation. All inhabitants of the earth will wor-
> ship the beast. (Rev. 13:7–8)

Using the power and alliances that he has built in the preceding three and a half years, the charismatic leader will consolidate his
authority over all the nations. His rule will not be limited just to
politics; he will take over the economy and religion as well.

8. Many Christians and Jews Who Refused to Worship the World Dictator Are Martyred (Rev. 7:9–17; 13:15)

Throughout this political and military upheaval, some people will
be persuaded by the events to worship Christ. These, sadly, who
were not believers in time to be raptured, will be persecuted and
even killed for following the one true faith instead of the Antichrist's
Babylonian religion.

> The second beast was given power to give breath
> to the image of the first beast, so that the image
> could speak and cause all who refused to worship
> the image to be killed. (Rev. 13:15)

9. Catastrophic Divine Judgments Represented by Seals, Trumpets, and Bowls Poured Out on the Earth (Rev. 6–18)

As bad as the tribulation has been up to this point, it still has room
to get worse. God will unleash cosmic catastrophes on the entire
earth.

> There was a great earthquake. The sun turned black
> like sackcloth made of goat hair, the whole moon
> turned blood red, and the stars in the sky fell to
> earth, as figs drop from a fig tree when shaken by
> a strong wind. The heavens receded like a scroll
> being rolled up, and every mountain and island was
> removed from its place. (Rev. 6:12–14)

The earth will experience physical, geological consequences of God's wrath and judgment.

10. World War Breaks Out Focusing on the Middle East: Battle of Armageddon (Dan. 11:40–45; Rev. 9:13–21; 16:12–16)

While most will quake in fear at the physical destruction around them, the Antichrist will take it as an opportunity to crush all who are not in thrall to him.

> He will invade many countries and sweep through
> them like a flood. He will also invade the Beautiful
> Land. Many countries will fall. (Dan. 11:40–41)

11. Babylon Destroyed (Rev. 18)

For all his plotting, and his political and military might, the Antichrist is still under the sovereign plan of God. All his striving and grasping for authority will ultimately serve only to be the final sign of Jesus Christ's second coming. The capital of his kingdom, the metaphorical Babylon, will be destroyed.

Then a mighty angel picked up a boulder the size of
a large millstone and threw it into the sea, and said:

"With such violence
  the great city of Babylon will be thrown down,
  never to be found again." (Rev. 18:21)

12. Second Coming of Christ (Matt. 24:27–31; Rev. 19:11–21)

Finally! The blessed and awaited event will happen. Christ will come
down in His full power and authority.

> Then will appear the sign of the Son of Man in
> heaven. And then all the peoples of the earth will
> mourn when they see the Son of Man coming on
> the clouds of heaven, with power and great glory.
> And he will send his angels with a loud trumpet
> call, and they will gather his elect from the four
> winds, from one end of the heavens to the other.
> (Matt. 24:30–31)

The earth will "mourn" because by this time all of Christ's believers will have been either raptured or martyred. The people left on
earth will be those who have rejected Christ. This will lead to the
next event.

13. Judgment of Wicked Jews and Gentiles (Ezek. 20:33–38; Matt. 25:31–46; Jude vv. 14–15; Rev. 19:15–21; 20:1–4)

This is not the ultimate judgment of believers. This is an earthly judgment of the wicked, preliminary to Christ's "great white throne judgment" of the living and the dead.

> See, the Lord is coming with thousands upon thousands of his holy ones to judge everyone, and to convict all of them of all the ungodly acts they have committed in their ungodliness, and of all the defiant words ungodly sinners have spoken against him. (Jude vv. 14–15)

14. Satan Bound for One Thousand Years (Rev. 20:1–3)

When Christ comes at the end of the tribulation, He will judge the living who have survived the catastrophes. He will also judge Satan himself, keeping him out of trouble during Christ's millennial kingdom.

> And I saw an angel coming down out of heaven, having the key to the Abyss and holding in his hand a great chain. He seized the dragon, that ancient serpent, who is the devil, or Satan, and bound him for a thousand years. (Rev. 20:1–2)

15. Resurrection of Tribulation Saints and Old Testament Saints (Dan. 12:2; Rev. 20:4)

With all the wicked (people and demons) out of the way, Christ will now resurrect those faithful who had died before this time.

> Multitudes who sleep in the dust of the earth will
> awake: some to everlasting life, others to shame and
> everlasting contempt. (Dan. 12:2)

16. Millennial Kingdom Begins (Rev. 20:5–6)

Together with Christ, all the resurrected faithful will live and rule
with their Lord in God's predicted glorious kingdom. This will be a
time of peace, righteousness, and spiritual prosperity for all believers.

> Blessed and holy are those who share in the first resur-
> rection. The second death has no power over them,
> but they will be priests of God and of Christ and will
> reign with him for a thousand years. (Rev. 20:6)

17. Final Rebellion at the End of the Millennium (Rev. 20:7–10)

After one thousand years of peace, Satan will have one final opportunity to work deception on God's people.

> When the thousand years are over, Satan will
> be released from his prison and will go out to
> deceive the nations in the four corners of the
> earth—Gog and Magog—and to gather them for
> battle. (Rev. 20:7–8)

This will be the last earthly battle. And while Satan might
think this his final chance for victory, in truth it will only be the
final step before Christ's ultimate judgment and the beginning of
His eternal reign in heaven.

18. Resurrection and Final Judgment of the Wicked: Great White Throne Judgment (Rev. 20:11–15)

At this time, all beings will be judged—human and demon, believers and unbelievers, living and dead. All will be under the authority of Christ on His heavenly throne.

> Then I saw a great white throne and him who was seated on it. The earth and the heavens fled from his presence, and there was no place for them. And I saw the dead, great and small, standing before the throne, and books were opened. Another book was opened, which is the book of life. The dead were judged according to what they had done as recorded in the books. (Rev. 20:11–12)

This is the last moment for the "old heaven" and the "old earth." All things that have been will now pass away.

19. Eternity Begins: New Heaven, New Earth, New Jerusalem (Rev. 21:1–4)

The eternal life that Jesus promised us will finally begin. And in this new place there will be no sadness or grief.

> Then I saw "a new heaven and a new earth," for the first heaven and the first earth had passed away, and there was no longer any sea. I saw the Holy City, the new Jerusalem, coming down out of heaven from God, prepared as a bride beautifully dressed

for her husband. And I heard a loud voice from the throne saying, "Look! God's dwelling place is now among the people, and he will dwell with them. They will be his people, and God himself will be with them and be their God." (Rev. 21:1–3)

We will finally be restored to our original, unbroken relationship with God that we had in the garden of Eden. We will walk with Him, and we will never be separated from our God again.

As you can see, many significant events transpire. But remember, these prophecies were meant not to confuse God's believers but to give us hope and secure knowledge of God's promises. May these prophecies encourage you as you learn more about them in the pages ahead.

2

WHAT IS THE RAPTURE?

When you hear the word *rapture*, what comes to mind? There is perhaps no other word in Scripture shrouded in such mystery. Beliefs regarding the rapture differ from church to church, believer to believer. But it doesn't have to be a confusing or intimidating topic. In fact, having a sound understanding of the rapture can enhance one's faith and strengthen one's relationship with God.

The original meaning of the word *rapture* is "great joy." Indeed, the rapture will be a great joy to those found in Christ. Hollywood portrayals of the rapture focus on the bewilderment of unbelievers when multitudes of people suddenly disappear. But that's an incomplete picture of the event. The passages in this chapter will shed light on what the Bible tells us about this mysterious yet hopeful event of the end times.

THE DAY OF CHRIST

... on the day of Christ. (Phil. 2:16)

The day of Christ in Scripture needs to be distinguished from the more common expression "the day of the Lord." The day of the

Lord normally has in view an extended period of time in which God deals in direct judgment on the world. This is developed, for instance, in 1 Thessalonians 5. The day of Christ, which is referred to with various wordings, refers to the rapture itself and the immediate results of the rapture and, therefore, does not deal with judgment on the world.

In 1 Corinthians 1:7–8, Paul stated, "Therefore you do not lack any spiritual gift as you eagerly wait for our Lord Jesus Christ to be revealed. He will also keep you firm to the end, so that you will be blameless on the day of our Lord Jesus Christ."

The reference in 1 Corinthians 5:5 is in the context of the rapture of the church, though the expression used is the more common phrase "the day of the Lord." Philippians 1:6 uses "the day of Christ Jesus," and Philippians 1:10 says "the day of Christ." In Philippians 2:16, the familiar expression "the day of Christ" again is used in reference to the rapture.

Though the varied wording does not in itself specify what day is in view, the context of these references indicates a connection to the rapture rather than to the day of the Lord, which will begin at the rapture of the church and extend through the tribulation and through the millennial kingdom, climaxing at the end of the millennium. Paul had confidence that God, who had begun a good work in the Philippian church, would continue His work until the day of the rapture and that the Philippian church would be found "pure and blameless for the day of Christ" (1:10). As the rapture of the church removes the church from the world, it will be followed immediately by the judgment seat of Christ in heaven when the works of believers will be evaluated and rewarded.

THE TIMING OF THE RAPTURE

> For God did not appoint us to suffer wrath but to
> receive salvation through our Lord Jesus Christ.
> (1 Thess. 5:9)

The day of the Lord will begin as a time period at the rapture, but its major events will not occur immediately. The ten-nation kingdom must be formed in the final seven years before the second coming will begin. Because the day of the Lord will start at the time of the rapture, the two events are linked as both beginning without warning and coming without a specific sign. However, once the day of the Lord begins, as it will after the rapture, and as time progresses, there will be obvious signs that the world is in the day of the Lord and in the period leading up to the second coming, just as there will be obvious evidences that the millennial kingdom has begun after the second coming. As the rapture must precede the signs, it necessarily must occur when the day of the Lord begins. (For further discussion, see 2 Thessalonians 2.)

One of the important signs of the day of the Lord is the fact that the people will be saying, "Peace and safety," when, as a matter of fact, "destruction will come on them suddenly, as labor pains on a pregnant woman, and they will not escape" (1 Thess. 5:3). The interpretation that this is the period between the rapture and the second coming seems most convincing. According to Daniel 9:27, there will be a seven-year period leading up to the second coming of Christ. The first half of this period will be a time when a covenant of peace will be made with Israel, as indicated in Daniel 9:27. During this period, people will hail peace as having been achieved, as mentioned in 1 Thessalonians 5:3. Then suddenly the great tribulation will begin and they will not escape its judgment. The world-shaking judgments that precede the second coming are described graphically in Revelation 6–18.

Because Christians are forewarned that the day of the Lord is coming, they should not be surprised and should live in the light of God's divine revelation. "But you, brothers and sisters, are not in darkness so that this day should surprise you like a thief. You are all children of the light and children of the day. We do not belong to the night or to the darkness" (1 Thess. 5:4–5). The day of the Lord is pictured here as a time of night for the world because it is a time of judgment, in contrast to the Christian's day, which is a time of light. The Christian's day will be climaxed by the rapture; the day for the wicked will begin at that time, and the judgments related to the day of the Lord will take place according to the time sequence of this period, with the great judgments occurring in the great tribulation and climaxing in the second coming. (Further descriptions of the day of the Lord are found in Isaiah 13:9–11 and Zephaniah 1:14–18; 3:4–15.)

As for the destinies of those who will be saved at the time of the rapture and those who are not brought out, "God did not appoint us to suffer wrath but to receive salvation through our Lord Jesus Christ" (1 Thess. 5:9). For Christians, their appointment is the rapture; for the unsaved, their appointment is the day of the Lord.

Paul realized that some Christians would have died before the rapture and that others would still be living. Accordingly, he said of Christ, "He died for us so that, whether we are awake or asleep, we may live together with him" (1 Thess. 5:10). By "awake," he was referring to Christians being still alive in the world; by "asleep," to the fact that Christians have died and their bodies will be "sleeping" in the grave though their souls are in heaven. His conclusion here, as in the other prophetic truths revealed in 1 Thessalonians, was a practical one: "Therefore encourage one another and build each other up, just as in fact you are doing" (v. 11).

THE FIRST PROMISE OF THE RAPTURE

> Do not let your hearts be troubled. You believe in God; believe also in me. My Father's house has many rooms; if that were not so, would I have told you that I am going there to prepare a place for you? And if I go and prepare a place for you, I will come back and take you to be with me that you also may be where I am. (John 14:1–3)

When they first heard that Jesus was going away, the apostles reacted immediately with fear and concern. With this comforting promise, Jesus described the rapture to His closest followers to assuage their fears. In light of His departure, Jesus promised them that He would return.

This was an entirely new revelation to be contrasted to Christ's earlier revelation concerning His second coming to judge the world. The newly mentioned purpose was to remove them from the world and take them to the Father's house, which clearly refers to heaven, where Jesus has gone before to prepare a place for those who believe in Him. This is the first reference in the New Testament to what Paul later referred to as the rapture of the church, as you will see in the next two prophecies.

THE REVEALING OF THE RAPTURE

> Brothers and sisters, we do not want you to be uninformed about those who sleep in death, so that you do not grieve like the rest of mankind, who have no hope.... For the Lord himself will come down from heaven, with a loud command, with the voice of the archangel and with the trumpet call of God, and the dead in Christ will rise first. After that, we who are still alive and are left will be caught up together with them in the clouds to meet the Lord in the air. And so we will be with the Lord forever. (1 Thess. 4:13, 16–17)

Taking its place alongside 1 Corinthians 15:51–58, the 1 Thessalonians 4:13–18 passage becomes one of the crucial revelations in regard to the rapture of the church. Though the Old Testament and the Synoptic Gospels reveal much concerning the second coming of Christ, the specific revelation concerning Christ's coming to take His church out of the world, both living and dead, was not revealed until John 14:1–3, the night before His crucifixion. Because the apostles at that time did not understand the difference between the first and second comings of Christ, they could hardly be instructed in the difference between the rapture of the church and Christ's second coming to judge and rule over the earth. A careful study of the passage in 1 Thessalonians 4 will do much to set the matter in its proper biblical revelation.

Unlike passages that deal with the second coming of Christ and trace the tremendous world-shaking events that will take place in the years preceding it, the rapture of the church is always presented as the next event and, as such, one that is not dependent on immediate preceding events. The rapture of the church, defined in 1 Thessalonians 4:17 as being "caught up together with them in the clouds to meet the Lord in the air," is a wonderful truth designed especially to encourage Christians.

Paul stated that he did not want the Thessalonians to be uninformed or ignorant concerning Christians who had died. As such, they were not to grieve for them as the world did, having no hope. In this passage, as in all scriptures, the sad lot of those who leave this world without faith in Christ is described in absolute terms of having "no hope" (v. 13). Only in Christ can one have hope of life to come in heaven.

Verse 14 states the nature of their faith in Christ that prompts them to believe that they will be ready when Christ comes: "We believe that Jesus died and rose again, and so we believe that God will bring with Jesus those who have fallen asleep in him."

If we can accept the supernatural event of Christ's dying for sin and rising from the grave, we can also believe in the future rapture of the church. This is defined as faith "that God will bring with Jesus those who have fallen asleep in him" (v. 14). At the rapture, believers are caught up to heaven. At the second coming, believers remain on earth. Accordingly, the event that Paul was describing here is quite different from the second coming of Christ as it is normally defined.

In what sense will Jesus bring with Him those who have fallen asleep? This refers to Christians who have died, and the expression of falling asleep is used to emphasize the fact that their deaths are temporary. When Christians die, their souls go immediately to heaven (2 Cor. 5:6–8). Paul declared that Jesus would bring with Him the souls of those who have fallen asleep. The purpose is brought out for this in the next verses: Jesus will cause their bodies to be raised from the dead and their souls will reenter their bodies (1 Thess. 4:15–16).

The actual sequence of events was described by Paul:

> According to the Lord's word, we tell you that we who are still alive, who are left until the coming of the Lord, will certainly not precede those who have fallen asleep. For the Lord himself will come down from heaven, with a loud command, with the voice of the archangel and with the trumpet call of God, and the dead in Christ will rise first. After that, we who are still alive and are left will be caught up together with them in the clouds to meet the Lord in the air. And so we will be with the Lord forever. (1 Thess. 4:15–17)

One question the Thessalonians seemed to face was this: If the Lord came for the living, would they have to wait before they could see those who were resurrected from the dead? Paul addressed this thought when he stated, "We who are still alive, who are left until the coming of the Lord, will certainly not precede those who have fallen asleep" (1 Thess. 4:15). In verse 16, the sequence of events is described. The Lord Jesus Himself will come down from heaven; that is, there will be a bodily return to earth. Jesus will utter a loud command related to the resurrection of the dead and the translation of the living. This will be accompanied by the voice of the archangel, which will be followed by the trumpet call of God. When this sounds, the event will take place. Christians who have died will rise first. Then Christians still living will be translated into bodies suited for heaven and "caught up together with them in the clouds to meet the Lord in the air" (v. 17).

For all practical purposes, these events will take place at the same time. Those living on earth who are translated will not have to wait for the resurrection of Christians who have died because those who are deceased will be resurrected a moment before. In expressing the thought that those who "are left will be caught up together with them in the clouds" (v. 17), Paul was revealing the essential character of the rapture, which is a snatching up or a bodily lifting up of those on earth, whether living or resurrected; their meeting the Lord in the air; and then their triumphant return to heaven. The event is described as being "with the Lord forever" (v. 17).

This is in keeping with the original revelation of the rapture in John 14:1–3, in which Christ informed His disciples that He would return for them to take them to the Father's house in heaven. They will remain in heaven until the great events in the period preceding the second coming of Christ take place, and the church in heaven will participate in the grand procession described in Revelation 19 of Christ's return to earth to set up His earthly kingdom.

The mention of clouds (1 Thess. 4:17) is taken by some to be literal clouds, as was true of Christ's ascension (Acts 1:9). Some believe the great number of those raptured will resemble a cloud, similar to the reference of Hebrews 12:1. The glorious prospect is that once this takes place, there will be no more separations between Christ and His church.

The locale of the church's future is not permanent, as they will be in heaven during the time preceding the second coming. They will be on earth during the millennial kingdom and then will inhabit the new heaven and new earth in eternity. In each of these situations, they will be with Christ in keeping with the symbolism of their marriage to Him as the heavenly Bridegroom.

Most significant in this passage is the fact that there are no preceding events, that is, no world-shaking events described as leading up to this event. In fact, the church down through the centuries expected the rapture to happen at any time, a hope that continues today. By contrast, the second coming of Christ will be preceded by divine judgments on the world and followed by the establishing of Christ's earthly kingdom. No mention is made of that here, but the emphasis is placed on the wonderful fellowship Christians will enjoy with the Savior. The wonderful hope of the rapture of the church is a source of constant encouragement to those who put their trust in Him and are looking forward to His coming.

THE MYSTERY OF THE RAPTURE

> We will not all sleep, but we will all be changed—
> in a flash, in the twinkling of an eye, at the last

> trumpet. For the trumpet will sound, the dead will be raised imperishable, and we will be changed. For the perishable must clothe itself with the imperishable, and the mortal with immortality. When the perishable has been clothed with the imperishable, and the mortal with immortality, then the saying that is written will come true: "Death has been swallowed up in victory." (1 Cor. 15:51–54)

As is brought out in the doctrine of the rapture (1 Thess. 4:14–17), not only will living Christians be caught up to heaven without dying, but those Christians who have died will also be resurrected. Both will receive new bodies that are suited for heaven. As Paul stated, they will be imperishable and will never be subject to decay, and they will be immortal, not subject to death (1 Cor. 15:53). They will also be free from sin and be the objects of God's grace and blessing throughout eternity.

The rapture of the church will mark a victory over death and the grave. Paul said, "Death has been swallowed up in victory. 'Where, O death, is your victory? Where, O death, is your sting?'" (1 Cor. 15:54–55). Paul was quoting from Isaiah 25:8, which states that God will "swallow up death forever," and from Hosea 13:14, in which God said, "I will deliver this people from the power of the grave; I will redeem them from death. Where, O death, are your plagues? Where, O grave, is your destruction?" This doctrine is stated with greater clarity in the New Testament as Paul traced the victory through Jesus Christ: "But thanks be to God! He gives us the victory through our Lord Jesus Christ" (1 Cor. 15:57).

In light of the great doctrine of the resurrection and the imminent hope of the Lord's return, believers are exhorted to make the most of their remaining time on earth. Paul continued, "Therefore, my dear brothers and sisters, stand firm. Let nothing move you. Always give yourselves fully to the work of the Lord, because you know that your labor in the Lord is not in vain" (v. 58). Believers should stand firm because we are standing on the rock Christ Jesus and on the sure promises of God. We should not allow the vicissitudes of life and the sorrows and burdens that come to move us away from confidence in God. While living out our lives on earth, we are to engage in the work of the Lord always as to time and fully as to extent, because we know that following this life at the judgment seat of Christ we will be rewarded and our "labor in the Lord is not in vain" (v. 58). This passage (1 Cor. 15:51–58) dealing with the rapture of the church coupled with Paul's earlier revelation of the Thessalonians (1 Thess. 4:14–17) constitute the principal scriptures on this great truth of the Lord's coming and the bright hope that it could be soon.

CHRIST APPEARS TO BELIEVERS FIRST

> In the sight of God, who gives life to everything, and of Christ Jesus …, I charge you to keep this command without spot or blame until the appearing of our Lord Jesus Christ, which God will bring about in his own time. (1 Tim. 6:13–15)

In connection with Paul's charge to Timothy to obey God and to have his testimony "without spot or blame" (v. 14), Paul viewed the Lord Jesus Christ as the final judge of this situation, who will judge Timothy at the time of His coming. Though Christ will not appear to the entire world until the time of His second coming, He obviously will appear to those who are raptured in the period before these end time events. At that time, Timothy's exemplary life will be evaluated. The Christian life has its completion at the time of Christ's coming.

THE HOPE OF BEING BROUGHT SAFELY TO CHRIST'S HEAVENLY KINGDOM

> For the grace of God ... teaches us to say "No" to ungodliness and worldly passions, and to live self-controlled, upright and godly lives in this present age, while we wait for the blessed hope—the appearing of the glory of our great God and Savior, Jesus Christ, who gave himself for us to redeem us from all wickedness and to purify for himself a people that are his very own, eager to do what is good. (Titus 2:11–14)

In appealing to Titus, Paul stated that the gospel of salvation "teaches us to say 'No' to ungodliness and worldly passions, and to live self-controlled, upright and godly lives in this present age" (v. 12). As we live our lives in this world, we have a wonderful hope. As Paul expressed it, "While we wait for the blessed hope—the appearing of the glory of our great God and Savior, Jesus Christ" (v. 13). This hope, obviously, related to the rapture of the church rather than the second coming of Christ to set up His kingdom, but the question has been raised as to why it is described as "the appearing of the glory."

At His second coming, Jesus will appear in a glorious event described in Revelation 19:11–16, an event that all the world will see (1:7). On the other hand, the rapture of the church is never described as visible to the world. The question therefore remains: How can the rapture be described as a glorious event, as an event that reveals the glory of God? The answer is quite simple.

While the world will not see the glory of Christ at the time of the rapture, as they will at the time of the second coming, at the rapture Christians will behold Him in His glory and to them it will be a glorious appearing. As stated in 1 John 3:2, "What we will be has not yet been made known. But we know that when Christ appears, we shall be like him, for we shall see him as he is."

Christians will necessarily need to be changed into bodies that are sinless in order to behold the Lord in His holy glory. The fact that we will "see him as he is" demonstrates that Christians will be transformed, which will make it possible for them to see Him in His glory.

CHRIST IS COMING TO RESCUE YOU

> In just a little while,
>> he who is coming will come
>> and will not delay. (Heb. 10:37)

As the Christian looks forward to relief from the present persecutions and difficulties, the promise is given, "In just a little while, he who is coming will come and will not delay" (v. 37). The reference, no doubt, is to the rapture of the church when every Christian, whether living or dead, will be caught up with the Lord. Necessarily, this will end the conflicts and problems of this life and constitute a part of the certain hope of Christians as we look to God to solve our problems.

CHRIST IS COMING SOON. TAKE HOPE!

> The end of all things is near. Therefore be alert and
> of sober mind so that you may pray. (1 Pet. 4:7)

In this brief statement, the fact that life will not go on forever should be an encouragement to Christians who are going through deep trouble. A Christian's pilgrimage on earth is temporary and soon may be cut short by the rapture of the church. This should serve as a stimulus to faithful service and endurance where persecutions and trials may be the lot of an individual Christian.

As these last few prophecies have shown us, the rapture is not meant to scare or cause us to lose sleep. Instead, the rapture offers hope. We may be suffering in this present world of brokenness and sin, but our Lord will not abandon us. He is coming back to take us away from this world, and we will truly experience the "great joy" that the word *rapture* originally intended.

3

THE ANTICHRIST AND TRIBULATION

As believers, we are called to be wise and shrewd in times of confusion. The more wayward the world becomes, the clearer our vision of truth should be. These visions serve as both a warning and guide as we compare them against the world we live in today. Although other biblical writers (the prophet Daniel in particular) referred to the rise of the Antichrist and events of the tribulation, John's visions as recorded in Revelation provide a thorough portrayal of the events following the rapture. Though not necessarily written in strict chronological order, Revelation provides a "road map" for us to follow.

USHERING IN THE ANTICHRIST AND THE TRIBULATION

Immediately after the rapture, there will be a season that could be called a period of preparation. In this period, a ten-nation group will form a political alliance in the Middle East. A leader will emerge who will gain control first of three and then of all ten (Dan. 7:8, 24–25). From this position of power, he will be able to enter into a covenant with Israel, bringing to rest the contentious relationship of Israel to its neighbors (9:27) and beginning the final seven-year countdown culminating in the second coming.

The first half of the seven years will be a time of peace as the covenant is observed. At the midpoint of the seven years, the covenant will be broken and the political leader will assume the position of ruler over the entire world. This will begin the period of persecution, the final three and a half years. The end of the dictator's reign at the second coming will be preceded by a great world war (Dan. 11:40–45; Rev. 16:14–16).

The three time periods between the rapture and the second coming of Christ, therefore, include an introductory period of unknown length, a period of peace of three and a half years, and a period of great persecution for three and a half years. The climax will be the second coming of Christ. Revelation 6–18 deals with the last seven years or, more specifically, the last three and a half years preceding the second coming.

THE EVENTS OF THE FIRST FOUR SEALS

John recorded the breaking of the first six seals in Revelation 6. The seven seals are the major events, or time periods, preceding the second coming. The results of each seal effect a crescendo of judgments coming with increased severity and intensifying tempo as the second coming approaches.

The opening of the first seal results in military conquest by a "world ruler" on a white horse. This will be the first major event of the tribulation.

John then addressed the breaking of the second seal, which revealed another horse and rider. John wrote, "When the Lamb opened the second seal, I heard the second living creature say, 'Come!' Then another horse came out, a fiery red one. Its rider was given power to take peace from the earth and to make people kill each other. To him was given a large sword" (vv. 3–4). The red horse is symbolic of war. And while this event does not refer to one specific war, it does mean that the last three and a half years will be a time of no peace.

The opening of the third seal reveals a rider on a black horse, known as famine. The aftermath of war, which apparently continues to some extent throughout this entire period, brings famine, especially in the areas where war has devastated crops.

The opening of the fourth seal marks the coming of the rider on a pale horse. The revelation of the pale horse is quite dramatic as it is actually an unearthly color, somewhat like a pale green, the same word being used in Mark 6:39 and Revelation 8:7. The rider is equally horrifying and is named "Death," and Hades follows close after. (Hades is the abode of those who die.) The most astounding part of the prophecy, however, is that these are given power over a fourth part of the earth, and instruments of death will include not only sword and famine, mentioned in the preceding seals, but also plague and the wild beasts of the earth.

These four horsemen represent the global nature of misery and destruction that will befall the world during the great tribulation. The Bible has much to say concerning this final great tribulation. In Daniel 9:27, the last half of the final seven years leading up to the second coming is the period in which the world ruler takes over and persecutes Israel and all who are not willing to obey him.

Christ added His word of explanation on the great tribulation: "For then there will be great distress, unequaled from the beginning of the world until now—and never to be equaled again. If those days had not been cut short, no one would survive, but for the sake of the elect those days will be shortened" (Matt. 24:21–22).

The distinguishing characteristic of the great tribulation is that it is an unprecedented time of trouble. Under this definition, the fourth seal qualifies because of the mass destruction of human life. In general, this passage of Scripture makes clear that the world is headed for extraordinary upheaval, but this will not occur until after the rapture of the church.

THE EVENTS OF THE FIFTH AND SIXTH SEALS

With the opening of the fifth seal, John saw the martyred dead from the tribulation (Rev. 6:9–11). They were asking how long it would be before they would be avenged, that is, when the great tribulation would end and the second coming would occur. They were given white robes and told there would be additional time during which some of their fellow servants and brothers would be killed.

The sixth seal resulted in a worldwide earthquake, when the sun turned black, the moon turned red, and the stars fell from the sky.

It would be difficult to paint a scene more dramatic and awful than that which is described in these verses. All the elements of catastrophic judgment are present: a great earthquake, the sun turning black, the moon becoming as blood, the stars of heaven falling like ripe figs, the heavens demonstrating major movements departing as a scroll, and every mountain and island moving. The picture of God's judgment on the world at this time is so dramatic that some recoil from it and attempt to interpret it in a less-than-literal sense. They would hold that this simply refers generally to political and social instability. However, the objections to a symbolic interpretation for which there is no norm or guiding principle are such that it is best to interpret these events in a literal sense.

In the light of the description of this terrible time of judgment, the prospect of the church being raptured before the time of wrath becomes all the more plausible and understandable. For the church to be forced to endure such a dramatic judgment can hardly be described as a blessed hope.

The question raised at the close of Revelation 6, "Who can withstand it?" (v. 17), makes clear that only those who respond to the grace of God will be able to have a victorious outcome. Whether it is fulfilled by the rapture of the church or whether it refers to those saved after the rapture who stand true, even to martyrdom, in this period of great tribulation, only those who are saved will conquer and be victorious.

THE TRUMPET WOES OF THE SEVENTH SEAL

When the seventh seal was opened, John saw seven angels with seven trumpets. As each angel blew his trumpet, another disaster occurred. These trumpet disasters are referred to as the seven woes of the seventh seal. The first trumpet caused hail and fire mixed with blood to rain on the earth, burning up one-third of the earth (Rev. 8).

The second trumpet caused an enormous mountain to be thrown into the sea, which destroyed one-third of the creatures in the sea and one-third of the ships on the sea. With the third trumpet, a great star fell from the sky and turned one-third of the freshwater on the earth bitter. The fourth trumpet darkened the sun, moon, and stars for one-third of the planet.

The next three trumpets were described as being even worse than the first four. As the fifth and sixth trumpets sound, a further judgment, more terrible than anything the people had experienced, comes to earth.

As John described:

> The fifth angel sounded his trumpet, and I saw a star that had fallen from the sky to the earth. The star was given the key to the shaft of the Abyss. When he opened the Abyss, smoke rose from it like the smoke from a gigantic furnace. The sun and sky were darkened by the smoke from the Abyss. And out of the smoke locusts came down on the earth and were given power like that of scorpions of the earth. They were told not to harm the grass of the earth or any plant or tree, but only those people who did not have the seal of God on their foreheads. They were not allowed to kill them but only to torture them for five months. And the agony they suffered was like that of the sting of a scorpion when it strikes. During those days people will seek death but will not find it; they will long to die, but death will elude them. (Rev. 9:1–6)

Further information is given on the nature of the locusts:

> The locusts looked like horses prepared for battle. On their heads they wore something like crowns of gold, and their faces resembled human faces. Their hair was like women's hair, and their teeth were like lions' teeth. They had breastplates like breastplates of iron, and the sound of their wings was like the thundering of many horses and chariots rushing into battle. They had tails with stingers, like scorpions, and in their tails they had power to torment people for five months. They had as king over them the angel of the Abyss, whose name in Hebrew is Abaddon and in Greek is Apollyon (that is, Destroyer). (vv. 7–11)

The sixth trumpet released four avenging angels (meaning demons) who killed one-third of humanity. (We will cover the seventh trumpet in the section "The Bowl Judgments of the Seventh Trumpet" later in this chapter.)

THE MINISTRY OF THE TWO WITNESSES

John then recorded the strange case of the two witnesses who were raised by God for this period (Rev. 11:1–13).

According to Scripture, the Holy City, Jerusalem, will be trampled underfoot of Gentiles for the final forty-two months preceding the second coming. This has actually been true ever since 600 BC, because from then to the time of the great tribulation, Israel never was in full possession of their holy places except by Gentile tolerance and permission. This is still true today as Israel could not retain its independence without the help of the United States. The forty-two months, however, refer to the great tribulation as a time when the holy place in the temple will be desecrated especially, and the great tribulation will run its course, climaxing in the second coming of Christ (Rev. 13:5). Though there have been brief periods in Israel's history when Israel temporarily retained control of the holy place, it will never be permanently theirs until the second coming of Christ.

John was then introduced to "two witnesses" (Rev. 11:3) who will be prophets in the end time. Their prophecy will cover 1,260 days, or forty-two months, the same length of time that the world ruler will possess the temple and turn it into a religious center for the worship of himself.

John described their unusual witness:

> "And I will appoint my two witnesses, and they will prophesy for 1,260 days, clothed in sackcloth." They are "the two olive trees" and the two lampstands, and "they stand before the Lord of the earth." If anyone tries to harm them, fire comes from their mouths and devours their enemies. This is how anyone who wants to harm them must die. They have power to shut up the heavens so that it will not rain during the time they are prophesying; and they have power to turn the waters into blood and to strike the earth with every kind of plague as often as they want. (Rev. 11:3–6)

The two witnesses, obviously, have unusual power comparable to that of Elijah and some of the other prophets, and they can inflict plagues much as Moses did in Egypt. Because of the unusual character of these two witnesses, a great deal of speculation has arisen about their identities. The Scriptures do not provide clues. Because Enoch and Elijah went to heaven without dying, some claim that these two witnesses are the prophets returned to earth. However, while the rule that it is appointed once to die was not observed in the case of Enoch and Elijah, it will be true of the entire church when it is raptured. Others attempt to relate the identities to Elijah and Moses because the power and ministry of the two witnesses are similar.

In view of the fact that the Bible does not indicate who they are, it is probably safe to recognize the two witnesses as appearing at the end time but who are not related to any previous historical characters.

The time then comes when God permits the witnesses to be overcome. John wrote:

> Now when they have finished their testimony, the beast that comes up from the Abyss will attack them, and overpower and kill them. Their bodies will lie in the public square of the great city—which is figuratively called Sodom and Egypt—where also their Lord was crucified. For three and a half days some from every people, tribe, language and nation will gaze on their bodies and refuse them burial. The inhabitants of the earth will gloat over them and will celebrate by sending each other gifts,

because these two prophets had tormented those
who live on the earth. (Rev. 11:7–10)

The question has been raised concerning the fact that the entire
world is able to gaze on their bodies though they actually are lying
in the street of Jerusalem. In the modern world with television and
online capabilities, this becomes something that could be easily fulfilled. Accordingly, all the greater the impact would be achieved if
their resurrection were also being broadcast at the time it took place.

John continued:

> But after the three and a half days the breath of
> life from God entered them, and they stood on
> their feet, and terror struck those who saw them.
> Then they heard a loud voice from heaven saying
> to them, "Come up here." And they went up to
> heaven in a cloud, while their enemies looked on.
>
> At that very hour there was a severe earthquake
> and a tenth of the city collapsed. Seven thousand
> people were killed in the earthquake, and the sur-
> vivors were terrified and gave glory to the God of
> heaven. (Rev. 11:11–13)

The resurrection of the two witnesses becomes an important
testimony at the time when the world is given to the worship of
the world ruler and Satan seems to be reigning supreme. Even
though God is permitting the terrible events of the great tribulation
to take place, including the catastrophes that will overtake most of

the human race, it is also evident that God is still in control and can provide a ministry of testimony to the world even under these circumstances.

THE COMING WORLD DICTATOR

In Revelation 13, prophecy focuses on the coming world government and the beast and the false prophet who lead it. The chapter opens with a revelation of the world ruler as the dragon standing "on the shore of the sea" contemplating the scene. John wrote, "And I saw a beast coming out of the sea. It had ten horns and seven heads, with ten crowns on its horns, and on each head a blasphemous name. The beast I saw resembled a leopard, but had feet like those of a bear and a mouth like that of a lion. The dragon gave the beast his power and his throne and great authority" (vv. 1–2).

The beast represents the revived Roman Empire and its ruler in the end times. Revelation here corresponds to the description given in Daniel 7:7–8 and Revelation 12:3; 17:3, 7. This passage makes plain that the beast, the future world ruler, will come out of the Mediterranean situation, with the sea representing the mass of humanity.

The empire is seen here in the form it will take after three of the initial ten nations are overthrown and come under the power of the beast (Dan. 7:8). The ten horns represent ten governments, as the horn is the symbol of political power. The crowns are diadems, or the emblems of governmental authority. Their blasphemous names indicate that they are opposed to God. Scholars interpret the seven heads in various ways, sometimes phases of government that precede, but more likely referring to the principal authorities that head these future governments.

John recorded, "The beast I saw resembled a leopard, but had feet like those of a bear and a mouth like that of a lion" (Rev. 13:2). In Daniel's description of the four great world empires preceding the kingdom from heaven, the four great empires are presented as beasts (Dan. 7). The Babylonian power was described as the lion (v. 4), the Medo-Persian Empire as the bear (v. 5), the leopard was Alexander the Great in his conquest (v. 6), and the beast of Revelation 13:1–8 (not named in Daniel 7:7) represented the future Roman Empire.

The first three of these empires, of course, are fulfilled prophecy—now history—with the first two of them observed by Daniel himself. Though some attempt other explanations, the only empire since that of Alexander worthy of consideration is the Roman Empire, by far the greatest of all empires of the ancient world and one with the longest history as a world power and one with the greatest influence on subsequent civilization.

The point in having these three animals represented in the beast of the sea is that the final world ruler gathers into his power all the power of the preceding rulers and their territories, and as the Scriptures go on to teach, eventually he becomes ruler over the entire globe, something that has never been accomplished.

John also pointed out, "The dragon gave the beast his power and his throne and great authority" (Rev 13:2). Behind the political government of the end time and its world rule is the power of Satan himself. The human world ruler is representative of Satan, much as Christ is the representative of God the Father. The final political power therefore is evil and opposed to everything that stands for the things of God.

John also gave a description of the beast and his worship and introduced some revelation that has caused a great deal of discussion. He wrote, "One of the heads of the beast seemed to have had a fatal wound, but the fatal wound had been healed. The whole world was filled with wonder and followed the beast. People worshiped the dragon because he had given authority to the beast, and they also worshiped the beast and asked, 'Who is like the beast? Who can wage war against it?'" (vv. 3–4).

Because a supernatural element is involved in the beast's rule and supplemented by the supernatural power of Satan, some ask whether anyone is equal to the beast and can make war with him. It is out of this background that the world worships the man and also worships Satan. The final form of apostasy and departure from God is to worship a man instead of God and to worship Satan, who sought to be like God (Isa. 14:14).

In the background of this description of the beast and the declaration that no one is able to stand against him, there may be a fulfillment of Ezekiel 38–39 with a great war as Russia and her allies attack Israel from the north, only to be destroyed. With Russia probably the leading world power, or at least in the Middle East, its destruction, as described in Ezekiel 38–39, would remove the only great military power in the world at the time. There is no indication that countries in the western hemisphere, such as the United States, would come into play at this time, and it is probable that they would now have less political power than they previously had.

Like the rulers of the great empires of the past, and in particular those who headed up the Roman Empire who are described as having "blasphemous names" (see Rev. 13:1), so the final ruler, a Gentile power, will engage in blasphemy against God. John wrote, "[The beast] opened its mouth to blaspheme God, and to slander his name and his dwelling place and those who live in heaven" (v. 6).

The extent of the beast's power is stated next. "It was given power to wage war against God's holy people and to conquer them. And it was given authority over every tribe, people, language and nation" (v. 7). The Scriptures leave no doubt that this is an actual political government that extends over the entire globe. This, of course, is in keeping with what Daniel predicted when he stated that the final world ruler "will devour the whole earth, trampling it down and crushing it" (Dan. 7:23). During most of the final three and a half years, the world ruler has power to cause the saints to be martyred, as previously revealed in Revelation 7:9–17. Enforcing his position as leader, he is worshipped as God: "All inhabitants of the earth will worship the beast—all whose names have not been written in the Lamb's book of life, the Lamb who was slain from the creation of the world" (13:8).

THE BOWL JUDGMENTS OF THE SEVENTH TRUMPET

The order of events involves rapid increase in severity and in frequency of the judgments of God, with the emphasis being on the seventh seal, the seven trumpets, and the seven bowls of the wrath of God (Rev. 15–16). As part of the blowing of the seventh trumpet, seven angels came out bearing seven golden bowls—each bowl bearing a plague of God's wrath. Because the seven bowls of the wrath of God are similar to the judgments of the trumpets and those of the seals, expositors have been tempted to equate them. Careful attention to the details, however, will point out the differences.

In obedience to the voice from the temple, the first angel pours out his bowl. As John recorded, "The first angel went and poured out his bowl on the land, and ugly, festering sores broke out on the people who had the mark of the beast and worshiped its image" (Rev. 16:2). By contrast, at the sound of the first trumpet, a third of the earth is burned up (8:7). In the first bowl of the wrath of God, worshippers of the beast are afflicted with painful sores, an experience similar to that of the Egyptians in Exodus 9:9–11. The only ones who escape this judgment are those who have refused to worship the beast.

Next, the second bowl is poured out. "The second angel poured out his bowl on the sea, and it turned into blood like that of a dead person, and every living thing in the sea died" (Rev. 16:3). At the sound of the second trumpet, a third of the sea turns to blood (8:8). This judgment again seems similar to the judgment of the plagues in Egypt (Exod. 7:20–25), which affected the River Nile, making it impossible to drink and killing the fish in the river. In reference to the sea, it is possible that it may be limited to the Mediterranean, but the same word would be used if the entire world were involved.

John then recorded the pouring out of the third bowl. "The third angel poured out his bowl on the rivers and springs of water, and they became blood" (Rev. 16:4). This is followed by the fourth bowl: "The fourth angel poured out his bowl on the sun, and the sun was allowed to scorch people with fire. They were seared by the intense heat and they cursed the name of God, who had control over these plagues, but they refused to repent and glorify him" (vv. 8–9). Similarities and contrasts can be seen again between the fourth trumpet and the fourth bowl. The fourth bowl relates only to the sun and increases the sun's intensity, whereas the fourth trumpet darkened a third of the sun, moon, and stars (8:12). Though the sphere of the judgment is the same, the effect is different.

The fifth bowl is announced. "The fifth angel poured out his bowl on the throne of the beast, and its kingdom was plunged into darkness. People gnawed their tongues in agony and cursed the God of heaven because of their pains and their sores, but they refused to repent of what they had done" (Rev. 16:10–11). This judgment apparently increases the severity of the affliction of the first bowl and describes those associated with the beast, and others as well, as being in unusual agony. The familiar theme of failure to repent is repeated here (see 2:21; 9:20–21). When the wicked are confronted with the power of God, they do not easily come to the place of repentance, but instead increase their rebellion against God.

The sixth bowl introduces a number of interesting facts. "The sixth angel poured out his bowl on the great river Euphrates, and its water was dried up to prepare the way for the kings from the East" (Rev. 16:12). When the sixth bowl is poured out, the time of the second coming is very near. One of the major features of the period just before the second coming is a world war in which various regions rebel against the world ruler who has taken power as the dictator. In the light of this military conclusion to the great tribulation, the sixth bowl makes its own contribution in preparing the way for the kings of the East to cross the Euphrates.

Few portions of Revelation have called for more varied interpretation than this verse. A survey of a hundred commentaries on Revelation reveals fifty different theories, practically all trying to interpret what is meant by the "kings from the East" and also to determine whether the Euphrates River is meant literally. The numerous symbolic interpretations are their own confession that symbolism is not the proper explanation.

Accordingly, a literal interpretation of the phrase is exactly what the text calls for, namely, that the Euphrates River will be dried up and this will prepare for military invasion by the kings of the East, probably including rulers of China and other countries.

The implication from the text is that this is accomplished by supernatural means, such as an earthquake, though the method is not revealed. In the twentieth century, however, Russia has helped build a series of dams across the Euphrates River to capture water for irrigation purposes. The fact is that at certain times in the season when all the water is stored, the Euphrates River is dry. If it were flowing at an ordinary rate, it would be a difficult river to cross because of the rough terrain on both sides of the river. But with the riverbed dry, a great army from the East could manage the crossing.

Though this passage does not connect directly with the sixth trumpet, apparently the sounding of that trumpet dries up the river to allow the great army of two hundred million to cross it (Rev. 9:14–16). The two events are chronologically close together even though they belong to different series.

Although no further information is given about the sixth bowl, John recorded a small parenthetic section giving the overview of Armageddon: "Then I saw three impure spirits that looked like frogs; they came out of the mouth of the dragon, out of the mouth of the beast and out of the mouth of the false prophet. They are demonic spirits that perform signs, and they go out to the kings of the whole world, to gather them for the battle on the great day of God Almighty" (Rev. 16:13–14).

This revelation is a combination of literal and symbolic. The evil spirits that look like frogs are actually fallen angels who, apparently, respond to the direction of the dragon that is Satan and the world ruler and his associate, the false prophet. The evil spirits are sent throughout the world to entice the kings of the world to join in the great world war that will be underway in the Holy Land.

Obviously, as long as the world government is intact, there will be no war. The fact that there is a war indicates rebellion against the rule of the world dictator toward the end of the great tribulation.

The gathering of the armies is in preparation for the second coming. Apparently Christ Himself proclaims the warning to be prepared, "Look, I come like a thief! Blessed is the one who stays awake and remains clothed, so as not to go naked and be shamefully exposed" (Rev. 16:15). Though many events precede the second coming and Satan himself is aware it is impending, many will be unprepared—"naked" and "shamefully exposed"—as far as God's righteousness is concerned.

The armies from the entire world are gathered geographically to the Holy Land, apparently to fight it out for power. The locale of the war is described as Armageddon. The term *Armageddon* geographically refers to the area eastward from Mount Megiddo in northern Israel and includes the large plain of Esdraelon. Megiddo is in the Hebrew a corresponding title to the Greek, Armageddon. This area has been the scene of great battles in the past, including that of Barak and the Canaanites (Judg. 4) and the victory of Gideon over the Midianites (Judg. 7). Saul and Josiah also were killed in this area. The valley is rather large, being fourteen miles wide and twenty miles long. Large as this area is, it obviously cannot contain the armies of millions of men, and it seems to be the marshaling point.

The enticement of the demons is apparently effective because the armies of the world assemble to fight it out in the Holy Land. The fact that the demons, along with the efforts of the dragon, the world ruler, and the false prophet, openly invite a world war seems to be a contradiction, because in Revelation 13 the world government is put together by Satan in order to fulfill his imitation of the millennial world government. Satan and the world ruler and the false prophet are a trilogy compared to the Father, Son, and Holy Spirit. Here, however, the same people are inviting countries of the world to fight it out, which appears to be a contradiction.

The answer to this puzzle is found in Revelation 19 as the second coming of Christ is revealed. What Satan is doing is gathering all the military power of the world in a vain effort to contend with the army from heaven. It, of course, is futile because Christ speaks the Word and the armies and their horses on both sides of the conflict are instantly killed in the awful judgment that occurs at the second coming.

With the announcement of the seventh bowl, the final judgments on the earth preceding the second coming are revealed: "The seventh angel poured out his bowl into the air, and out of the temple came a loud voice from the throne, saying, 'It is done!' Then there came flashes of lightning, rumblings, peals of thunder and a severe earthquake. No earthquake like it has ever occurred since mankind has been on earth, so tremendous was the quake" (Rev. 16:17–18).

Earthquakes have plagued the world throughout history. With increased population and building of cities, earthquakes now affect populous areas with increased casualties and destruction of property.

This final earthquake that occurs before the second coming of Christ eclipses all that have gone before.

This earthquake causes the destruction of the "great city," presumably Babylon, which represents the center of earthly power and religion. John further described the destruction of the world: "Every island fled away and the mountains could not be found. From the sky huge hailstones, each weighing about a hundred pounds, fell on people. And they cursed God on account of the plague of hail, because the plague was so terrible" (Rev. 16:20–21). The topographical nature of the world is dramatically changed, probably as a result of the aftermath of the earthquake with islands and mountains disappearing with resultant loss of life and property. Huge waves in the ocean created by these changes bring destruction that is beyond description.

In addition to the earthquake, there is a tremendous supernatural hailstorm with huge hailstones weighing approximately one hundred pounds each. Whatever is left from the earthquake in terms of man-made monuments is beaten to pulp by these huge blocks of ice. As in previous judgments of God, however, it does not bring repentance or confession of sin; instead, the people, recognizing that the judgments came from God, curse Him.

The world is now set for the second coming of Christ, but before this occurs, a parenthetic section dealing with Babylon is introduced.

THE DESTRUCTION OF BABYLON

Revelation 18 continues a prophetic revelation concerning Babylon but with the context and meaning of this chapter being entirely different from the preceding chapter. Revelation 17 is probably fulfilled before the great tribulation begins. By contrast, the events of Revelation 18 are probably fulfilled as a judgment at the time of the second coming of Christ.

Expositors have struggled with Revelation 17 and 18 in an attempt to find some reasonable explanation of the prophecies. Probably the best approach for Revelation 17 is to regard it as having its fulfillment in the world church movement that will be judged and destroyed three and a half years before the second coming of Christ.

Revelation 18, however, deals specifically with a city that is essentially a political entity. The question is: When will this prophecy be fulfilled?

The interpretation of this chapter depends on the question of whether Babylon will be rebuilt as the capital of the world in the end time or whether Babylon will be fulfilled by the role of Rome in the period preceding the second coming. The concept that the seven hills refer to the city of Rome is found to be unsupportable in the context, and the evidence that the city of Rome will be in some sense the Babylon represented here does not have sufficient basis of support in other scriptures to justify the conclusion. Accordingly, the approach taken here is to anticipate Babylon as a city that will be rebuilt as the capital of the final world empire and will be destroyed physically as well as politically at the time of the second coming.

This conclusion is based on studies of the Old Testament prophecies that point to the sudden and catastrophic destruction of Babylon (Isa. 13:5–6, 10, 19–22; 14:1–6, 22, 25–26; Jer. 51). These prophecies anticipating the destruction of Babylon were not fulfilled in history. When the Medes and the Persians took over Babylon in 539 BC, they did not destroy the city. The city of Babylon continued to be a population center through the time of Christ when there was a large colony of Jews living there. Actually, there was no act of sudden destruction, but Babylon did gradually diminish as a city in the centuries following the first coming of Christ until its current ruinous state today. Thus, the fulfillment of the promise in the Old Testament has not occurred. It is on this basis that some anticipate a rebuilt Babylon as a part of the world empire system prior to the second coming of Christ.

Revelation 18 fits into this picture well because it describes a sudden catastrophic destruction of the city and, with it, the termination of its political and commercial power. Presented as it is in connection with the second coming of Christ in the book of Revelation, the implication is that the Old Testament fall of Babylon did not fulfill all the prophecies.

The announcement given in Revelation 18 is by "another angel" than the one who revealed the destruction of Babylon in Revelation 17. John described this: "After this I saw another angel coming down from heaven. He had great authority, and the earth was illuminated by his splendor" (18:1). This angel came down after chapter 17 chronologically. In fact, the destruction of chapter 17 and the destruction of chapter 18 are two different events separated by three and a half years.

John recorded, "With a mighty voice he shouted: 'Fallen! Fallen is Babylon the Great! She has become a dwelling for demons and a haunt for every impure spirit, a haunt for every unclean bird, a haunt for every unclean and detestable animal. For all the nations have drunk the maddening wine of her adulteries. The kings of the earth committed adultery with her, and the merchants of the earth grew rich from her excessive luxuries'" (18:2–3). The fall of Babylon as prophesied here will be followed by being unpopulated, a center of demon power, and the home for wild animals. This has not occurred in the history of Babylon.

Scriptures are not clear whether the destruction of Babylon will occur immediately before the second coming or immediately after. According to Revelation 16:19, however, the great earthquake that precedes the second coming will destroy the cities of the Gentiles, and it could be that Babylon will be destroyed at the same time.

John then heard an additional revelation concerning the fall of Babylon:

> Then I heard another voice from heaven say:
>
> "Come out of her, my people,"
>> so that you will not share in her sins,
>> so that you will not receive any of her plagues;
> for her sins are piled up to heaven,
>> and God has remembered her crimes.
> Give back to her as she has given;
>> pay her back double for what she has done.
>> Pour her a double portion from her own cup.
> Give her as much torment and grief
>> as the glory and luxury she gave herself.
> In her heart she boasts,
>> "I sit enthroned as queen.
> I am not a widow;
>> I will never mourn."

Therefore in one day her plagues will overtake her:
    death, mourning and famine.
She will be consumed by fire,
    for mighty is the Lord God who judges her.
      (Rev. 18:4–8)

Christians living in Babylon in the end times will be urged to flee, much as the saved inhabitants of Babylon were urged to flee in the Old Testament (Jer. 50:4–9; 51:6). The warning lest the plagues overtake them would seem to indicate that this might be subsequent to the seventh bowl of the wrath of God (Rev. 16:17–21). The statement "her sins are piled up to heaven" (18:5) is a allusion to the Tower of Babel (Gen. 11:5–9), a reminder of how God judged the Tower of Babel when it began the long history of Babylon.

Another voice from heaven exhorted them to punish Babylon in keeping with its illicit sins and luxuries. Again, the judgment does not come in a long, drawn-out situation but by the immediate judgment on a given day. The exhortation to pay Babylon back double for what she has done is an application of the law of retribution. When it boasts that it is not a "widow," it has in mind all its illicit love affairs with the kings on earth. The result is that Babylon will be destroyed and burned with fire (Rev. 18:8).

The voice from heaven continued its revelation:

The merchants of the earth will weep and mourn over her because no one buys their cargoes anymore—cargoes of gold, silver, precious stones and pearls; fine linen, purple, silk and scarlet cloth; every sort of citron wood, and articles of every kind made of ivory, costly wood, bronze, iron and marble; cargoes of cinnamon and spice, of incense, myrrh and frankincense, of wine and olive oil, of fine flour and wheat; cattle and sheep; horses and carriages; and human beings sold as slaves.

They will say, "The fruit you longed for is gone from you. All your luxury and splendor have vanished, never to be recovered." The merchants who sold these things and gained their wealth from her will stand far off, terrified at her torment. They will weep and mourn and cry out:

"Woe! Woe to you, great city,
> dressed in fine linen, purple and scarlet,
> and glittering with gold, precious stones and
> > pearls!
In one hour such great wealth has been brought
> to ruin!" (Rev. 18:11–17)

This remarkable account of the products that were used by ancient Babylon indicates the extensive wealth of the city and the many costly things that were normally imported. As the city is destroyed, the merchants lament its passing, and the reminder is given that this destruction takes place "in one hour."

There is no correspondence of the scene here with what happened to Babylon in the Old Testament, and this gives further basis for belief that this is a future situation in which Babylon is rebuilt and then brought to ruin in connection with the second coming of Christ. The sea captains and merchants who had conveyed these rich products to Babylon also add their lament:

> Every sea captain, and all who travel by ship, the sailors, and all who earn their living from the sea, will stand far off. When they see the smoke of her burning, they will exclaim, "Was there ever a city like this great city?" They will throw dust on their heads, and with weeping and mourning cry out:

> "Woe! Woe to you, great city,
>   where all who had ships on the sea
>   became rich through her wealth!
> In one hour she has been brought to ruin!'"
>   (Rev. 18:17–19)

Some have suggested that the Euphrates at the time will be opened to sea traffic, which would account for the reference to ships and sailors.

Joining the cry over Babylon is heaven itself. As John stated, "Rejoice over her, you heavens! Rejoice, you people of God! Rejoice, apostles and prophets! For God has judged her with the judgment she imposed on you" (v. 20).

The final description of the destruction of Babylon comes after an angel throws a millstone into the sea, symbolic of the destruction of Babylon:

Then a mighty angel picked up a boulder the size of
a large millstone and threw it into the sea, and said:

"With such violence
    the great city of Babylon will be thrown down,
    never to be found again.
The music of harpists and musicians, pipers and
            trumpeters,
    will never be heard in you again.
No worker of any trade
    will ever be found in you again.
The sound of a millstone
    will never be heard in you again.
The light of a lamp
    will never shine in you again.
The voice of bridegroom and bride
    will never be heard in you again.
Your merchants were the world's important
            people.
    By your magic spell all the nations were led
    astray.
In her was found the blood of prophets and of
            God's holy people,
    of all who have been slaughtered on the
    earth." (vv. 21–24)

The prophecy is specific that life and events will come to
a total stop in the ancient city of Babylon because of a sudden

destruction that will come in one day. As this has not yet been fulfilled, it lends credence to the concept that Babylon will be rebuilt in the end time and then suffer this destruction at the time of the second coming.

4

THE KING'S RETURN: CHRIST'S SECOND COMING

In the midst of today's complex and confusing culture, it can be easy to think that God has forgotten us. After all, it has been two thousand years since Christ died and was resurrected. If He were going to come back, wouldn't He have done so by now? In fact, even the first generation of believers struggled with this question. They assumed Christ's second coming would happen during their lifetimes, and they became upset when they started to see their friends and fellow believers dying off. The apostles Paul and Peter had to teach the church quite a bit about the timing and certainty of Christ's coming.

Throughout the Old and New Testaments, the Bible is consistent about teaching that the Messiah will come in power, majesty, and authority over the earth. These prophecies are meant to help strengthen and edify our faith as we wait on the Lord.

WHAT IS THE DAY OF THE LORD?

Now, brothers and sisters, about times and dates we do not need to write to you, for you know very

> well that the day of the Lord will come like a thief
> in the night. While people are saying, "Peace and
> safety," destruction will come on them suddenly, as
> labor pains on a pregnant woman, and they will not
> escape. (1 Thess. 5:1–3)

In 1 Thessalonians 5:1–11, Paul connected the Old Testament concept of the "day of the Lord" to the rapture and second coming. Like a thief in the night, who comes without warning, the rapture will occur and the day of the Lord will begin.

Mentioned frequently in the Old Testament, the day of the Lord refers to any special period in which God intervenes supernaturally, bringing judgment on the world. An outstanding illustration is the book of Joel, which has as its theme the day of the Lord. The term is properly used of the crisis that occurred in the time of Joel brought on by the infestation of locusts, which ruined their crops, bringing starvation and destruction.

Joel described it: "Alas for that day! For the day of the Lord is near; it will come like destruction from the Almighty" (Joel 1:15). Verses 16–20 go on to graphically describe the devastating loss of crops. This, however, was not the only problem the people faced. They were also to experience the invading Assyrian armies, which would conquer them, much as the locusts had conquered them. They were experiencing a day of judgment from God.

The day described in Joel was not a long period of time, but it was longer than twenty-four hours. This impending day of the Lord fulfilled in the Old Testament was an appeal by Joel to the people of Israel to return to the Lord. Joel wrote:

"Even now," declares the LORD,
 "return to me with all your heart,
 with fasting and weeping and mourning."

Rend your heart
 and not your garments.
Return to the LORD your God,
 for he is gracious and compassionate,
slow to anger and abounding in love,
 and he relents from sending calamity.
Who knows? He may turn and relent
 and leave behind a blessing—
grain offerings and drink offerings
 for the LORD your God. (2:12–14)

The future period of God's intervention in the world will begin at the rapture and will include the period of trouble preceding the second coming of Christ and the establishment of God's kingdom on the earth. The day of the Lord will also include the millennial kingdom. The entire period before and after the second coming of Christ will constitute a special divine intervention and rule of righteousness on the earth in the way that is not being experienced in the present age.

The day of the Lord will begin as a time period at the rapture, but its major events will not start immediately. The ten-nation kingdom must be formed in the final seven years before the second coming will begin. Because the day of the Lord will begin as a time period at the time of the rapture, the two events are linked as both beginning without warning and coming without a specific sign. Once the day of the Lord begins, however, as it will after the rapture, over time there will be obvious signs that the world is in the day of the Lord and in the period leading up to the second coming, just as there will be obvious evidences that the millennial kingdom has begun after the second coming.

One of the important signs of the day of the Lord is that the people will be saying, "Peace and safety," when, as a matter of fact, "destruction will come on them suddenly, as labor pains on a pregnant woman, and they will not escape."

Because Christians have been told of the rapture, they should not be asleep but be alert and self-controlled. In contrast to the world, which drowns its sorrows in drinking (1 Thess. 5:7), a Christian should be self-controlled, "putting on faith and love as a breastplate, and the hope of salvation as a helmet" (v. 8).

WHEN IS THE DAY OF THE LORD?

In 1 Thessalonians 5, the apostle pointed out to the Thessalonians that the day of the Lord would begin at the time of the rapture and that it would be a time period in which God deals in direct judgment in the world before the second coming. In all this, God will deal directly with human sin, in contrast to His withholding judgment in the present age.

False teachers had come to the Thessalonians, however, and told them they were already in the day of the Lord, contradicting Paul's teaching, unsettling and alarming the Thessalonian church because they had understood Paul to say that they would not be in this period. Accordingly, Paul attempted to correct this difficulty by saying the major events of the day of the Lord had not occurred and there was no evidence that the day had already begun.

The problem was stated in the opening verses of 2 Thessalonians 2:

> Concerning the coming of our Lord Jesus Christ and our being gathered to him, we ask you, brothers and sisters, not to become easily unsettled or alarmed by the teaching allegedly from us— whether by a prophecy or by word of mouth or by letter—asserting that the day of the Lord has already come. Don't let anyone deceive you in any way, for that day will not come until the rebellion occurs and the man of lawlessness is revealed, the man doomed to destruction. He will oppose and will exalt himself over everything that is called God or is worshiped, so that he sets himself up in God's temple, proclaiming himself to be God. (vv. 1–4)

In approaching the interpretation of these verses, distinction must be made between the concept of the day of the Lord beginning at a specific moment and the major events of the day of the Lord coming that will occur some time after it has begun. The parallel is the ordinary twenty-four-hour period. The day actually begins at midnight, but no activity marks the day until one is raised from sleep to greet the morning. Then as the events of the day unfold, it is evident that a new day has come. The time period, accordingly, begins before the major events of the period come.

The same is true of the day of the Lord. The time period begins at the rapture of the church, but the major events do not come immediately. However, if the day of the Lord has progressed very far, there will be unmistakable signs that they are in the day of the Lord.

It is encouraging to know that we are not the first believers to be concerned about the timing of the end times. But Paul encouraged the Thessalonians—and now encourages us as well—to live as if Christ might come back at any moment. We are assured that we'll recognize the day of the Lord when it does truly happen.

ARE WE SURE ABOUT "DAY OF THE LORD"?

> Above all, you must understand that in the last days scoffers will come, scoffing and following their own evil desires. They will say, "Where is this 'coming' he promised? Ever since our ancestors died, everything goes on as it has since the beginning of creation." But they deliberately forget that long ago by God's word the heavens came into being and the earth was formed out of water and by water. By these waters also the world of that time was deluged and destroyed. By the same word the present heavens and earth are reserved for fire, being kept for the day of judgment and destruction of the ungodly. (2 Pet. 3:3–7)

Paul was not the only one needing to encourage believers in their doubt of the day of the Lord. The apostle Peter also had things to say on the subject. The letter of 2 Peter, written so shortly before Peter's martyrdom, anticipates that there will be worldwide scoffing about the second coming.

The argument of scoffers is that because of the uniformity of nature—that is, always acting according to natural law—there is no room for a miraculous event, like a person returning who had once died. They argue that although God created the world (a concession on the part of unbelievers), since then He has dealt with the world entirely on the basis of natural laws. As they put it, "everything goes on as it has since the beginning of creation" (v. 4).

These scoffers, however, have overlooked a great deal. If they are right, there is nothing to the accounts in the Bible of the many miracles that God performed, such as the miracle of the flood and of course the supernatural event of Jesus Christ becoming incarnate. Peter accused the scoffers of having a short memory and forgetting purposely: "But they deliberately forget that long ago by God's word the heavens came into being and the earth was formed out of water and by water" (v. 5). Though they passed by the question of the origin of all things by saying God created it, they failed to realize that this recognizes God has supernatural power over natural laws and can change some or all of them as He wills.

Peter also accused them of forgetting the historical fact of the flood. In 2 Peter 3:5, he mentioned that "the earth was formed out of water and by water," referring to the account of Genesis 1. However, in history there was added the account of Noah's flood when these same waters that were prominent in creation now covered the earth and destroyed it: "By these waters also the world of that time was deluged and destroyed" (v. 6). The same word of God, which predicted the flood and fulfilled it, also predicted that there would be no further flood and that the next destruction of the world will be by fire: "By the same word the present heavens and earth are reserved for fire, being kept for the day of judgment and destruction of the ungodly" (v. 7).

IS CHRIST WAITING TOO LONG FOR THE SECOND COMING?

> But do not forget this one thing, dear friends: With the Lord a day is like a thousand years, and a thousand years are like a day. The Lord is not slow in keeping his promise, as some understand slowness. Instead he is patient with you, not wanting anyone to perish, but everyone to come to repentance. (2 Pet. 3:8–9)

The fact is that the second coming of Christ did not occur immediately, as many of the early Christians probably anticipated. Here Peter introduced God's viewpoint of time as compared to man's: "But do not forget this one thing, dear friends: With the Lord a day is like a thousand years, and a thousand years are like a day" (v. 8). This verse is commonly misunderstood as meaning that a thousand years does not mean a thousand years. The contrast is not between literal meaning and nonliteral meaning, but between the view of God and the view of man. For God, who existed from all eternity past, a twenty-four-hour day could be like a thousand years of human history. If one attempted to write all the events of a single day—all that people did, all that animals did, all that occurred in the vegetable world, and everything else that happened in the other aspects of creation—it would be impossible to give a chronology of the work of one day. The facts of events in one day would be greater than a thousand years of human history as viewed by man. God looks at the world microscopically. He knows all about the tangled events that form a single twenty-four-hour day.

On the other hand, a thousand years of human history is also a brief time for God. When dealing with an infinite God who has always existed, one cannot argue with time factors. The passage of two thousand years since the first coming of Christ should not be any ground for viewing the second coming with uncertainty. As Peter expressed it, "The Lord is not slow in keeping his promise, as some understand slowness. Instead he is patient with you, not wanting anyone to perish, but everyone to come to repentance" (v. 9).

Instead of being inattentive and slow in responding to the promise of the second coming, God has a loving purpose in wanting to extend the message of salvation and forgiveness to more individuals before the time of judgment comes. In other words, God is waiting for those who have not heard to hear. He is waiting for those who have heard to respond. He does not desire to punish anyone with eternal punishment; He wants everyone to come to repentance.

Here we have the contrast between God's sovereign will and His desires. In the nature of a moral universe where people are given choices in creating the situation, God knew that not all would choose the right path. In His heart of love, which has provided grace for every person through Jesus Christ, God wants all to be saved and He wants to give them all the time that is possible to hear and respond to the message. The fact is that, regardless of when the Lord came, there would be many who did not believe. The situation will be similar to that of the days of Noah, using an illustration in Scripture (Matt. 24:37–39). Though the ark took more than one hundred years to build and Noah was faithful in telling people why it was being built, there seemed to be no response to his message except that from his own family; his three sons and their wives shared this faith. At the time of the second coming of Christ, some will not be ready, while others will be awaiting His coming.

Regardless of the timing, all scriptural accounts agree that at His second coming, Christ will have all the authority that belongs to Him as a person of the triune God.

CHRIST'S AUTHORITY AT THE SECOND COMING

> You have made them a little lower than the angels
>   and crowned them with glory and honor.
> You made them rulers over the works of your
>   hands;
>   you put everything under their feet.
>   (Ps. 8:5–6)

In Psalm 8, the habitation of Christ on earth is compared with the glory He had when He returned to heaven: "You [Lord] have made them a little lower than the angels and crowned them with glory and honor" (v. 5). As the book of Hebrews continues to treat this revelation, it is summarized: "In putting everything under them, God left nothing that is not subject to them. Yet at present we do not see everything subject to them" (2:8). Christ now has not realized subjection of the whole world, suffering death on the cross and being made "perfect through what he suffered" (v. 10). His right to rule is affirmed: "You made them rulers over the works of your hands; you put everything under their feet; all flocks and herds, and the animals of the wild, the birds in the sky, and the fish in the sea, all that swim the paths of the seas" (Ps. 8:6–8).

The contrast of Psalm 8 was between Christ and Adam. It was God's intent that Adam should rule the world, but this was interrupted by the entrance of sin into the situation. Now Christ has fulfilled what was originally Adam's responsibility. Having suffered on earth and gone through the humiliation of death, Christ now has been exalted to heaven, and it is God's purpose ultimately for Him to rule over the earth. This scripture will be fulfilled completely at Christ's second coming.

A COMING RIGHTEOUS KING

> "The days are coming," declares the LORD,
>> "when I will raise up for David a righteous
>> Branch,
> a King who will reign wisely
>> and do what is just and right in the land....
> This is the name by which he will be called:
>> The LORD Our Righteous Savior."
>> (Jer. 23:5–6)

Christ's coming as the King of Israel is clearly predicted in Jeremiah 23:1–8. The reference to Christ is made evident by the fact that He is called "the LORD Our Righteous Savior." No such event has been fulfilled in history, and it must be related, like many other passages, to the second coming of Christ.

THE SIGNS AND WONDERS OF THE SECOND COMING

> I will pour out my Spirit in those days.
> I will show wonders in the heavens
>   and on the earth,
>   blood and fire and billows of smoke.
> The sun will be turned to darkness
>   and the moon to blood
>   before the coming of the great and dreadful
>   day of the LORD. (Joel 2:29–31)

The apostle Peter quoted from Joel 2 in his Pentecostal sermon (Acts 2:14–21). It was quite clear that the entire prophecy of Joel was not fulfilled, but what Peter alluded to was the similarity of the situation. Just as in Joel's time, the people of Israel were called to repentance in the hope that the day of the Lord's blessing would come on them, so those who listened to Peter's Pentecostal sermon were exhorted to turn to the Lord in anticipation that the promised blessings might follow.

The length of the present church age was unknown to Peter and to everyone else at the time of his Pentecostal sermon. On the basis of existing scripture, he could rightfully expect the rapture to occur and the events following to come about immediately. This would include the dark days of the great tribulation described in Joel 2:30–31, which would precede the second coming of Christ and a time of blessing to follow.

The prophecy of Joel awaits complete fulfillment in relation to the second coming of Christ. It will include supernatural revelation and miraculous events in the heavens and on the earth and will open the day of salvation to all who call on the name of the Lord (see Rom. 10:13).

THE MILITARY IMPACT OF THE LORD'S SECOND COMING

> A day of the LORD is coming, Jerusalem, when your possessions will be plundered and divided up within your very walls.…
> Then the LORD will go out and fight against those nations, as he fights on a day of battle. (Zech. 14:1, 3)

The interpretation of this difficult portion of Zechariah 14 was made clear by later revelation concerning the events of the end time leading up to the second coming of Christ. The warfare and tragedy described in these verses are a prediction of the horrors that will occur during the great tribulation. But with Christ's second coming, He will "fight" on behalf of God's people and put an end to the strife, warfare, and persecution.

THE PHYSICAL IMPACT OF THE LORD'S SECOND COMING

> On that day his feet will stand on the Mount of
> Olives, east of Jerusalem, and the Mount of Olives
> will be split in two from east to west, forming a
> great valley, with half of the mountain moving
> north and half moving south....
>
> On that day there will be neither sunlight nor
> cold, frosty darkness. It will be a unique day—a
> day known only to the LORD—with no distinction
> between day and night. When evening comes, there
> will be light.
>
> On that day living water will flow out from
> Jerusalem, half of it east to the Dead Sea and half
> of it west to the Mediterranean Sea, in summer and
> in winter.
>
> The LORD will be king over the whole earth.
> On that day there will be one LORD, and his name
> the only name. (Zech. 14:4, 6–9)

Along with the second coming of Christ will be cataclysmic
events, including the division of the Mount of Olives into northern
and southern halves with the great valley between: "On that day his
feet will stand on the Mount of Olives, east of Jerusalem, and the
Mount of Olives will be split in two from east to west, forming a
great valley, with half of the mountain moving north and half moving south" (v. 4). Those who seek to escape Jerusalem will flee by

this newly made valley, which apparently will extend from Jerusalem down to the city of Jericho. This makes clear that the second coming is a future event, as the Mount of Olives is still intact.

That day will also be unique in that apparently it will be lengthened: "On that day there will be neither sunlight nor cold, frosty darkness. It will be a unique day—a day known only to the LORD—with no distinction between day and night. When evening comes, there will be light" (v. 6).

Topographical changes will take place to apparently elevate Jerusalem so waters flowing from it will go half to the eastern sea, or the Dead Sea, and half to the western sea, or the Mediterranean. And other unusual phenomena will occur in connection with the second coming of Christ (Isa. 11:10; 34:4; Joel 2:10, 30–31; 3:15; Matt. 24:29). A great many events are packed into a relatively short period of time.

SEPARATING THE RIGHTEOUS AND WICKED AT THE SECOND COMING

As always in times of apostasy, the majority may not serve God or honor Him, but there are always the godly few—in this case, a faithful remnant who walked with God (Mal. 3:16–4:3). They had written "a scroll of remembrance," listing those who feared the Lord and honored Him (3:16). "'On the day when I act,' says the LORD Almighty, 'they will be my treasured possession. I will spare them, just as a father has compassion and spares his son who serves him. And you will again see the distinction between the righteous and the wicked, between those who serve God and those who do not'" (vv. 17–18).

The distinction between the righteous and the wicked will be a feature of the day of the Lord that Malachi stated was coming (4:1). It will be a day that "'will burn like a furnace. All the arrogant and every evildoer will be stubble, and the day that is coming will set them on fire,' says the LORD Almighty." Further, God said, "Not a root or a branch will be left to them" (v. 1). This does not promise annihilation of the wicked, but it does indicate that any who are so wicked will be excluded from the kingdom.

While the day of the Lord will be a time of judgment on the wicked, it also will be a time when the righteous will be recognized: "But for you who revere my name, the sun of righteousness will rise with healing in its rays. And you will go out and frolic like well-fed calves" (v. 2). The wicked were represented as being trampled underfoot like ashes (v. 3). This answers completely the false statement of the wicked; but it does make a difference whether they serve God. In the ultimate judgment, the righteous will flourish and the wicked will suffer. This was fulfilled in history and will be fulfilled at the second coming.

THE JUDGMENT OF THE GENTILES AT THE SECOND COMING

> When the Son of Man comes in his glory, and all the angels with him, he will sit on his glorious throne. All the nations will be gathered before him, and he will separate the people one from another as a shepherd separates the sheep from the goats....
>
> Then they will go away to eternal punishment, but the righteous to eternal life. (Matt. 25:31–32, 46)

The judgment in Matthew 25:31–46 relating to the Gentiles at the time of the second coming is revealed only here in Scripture. Premillenarians contrast this judgment to several other judgments mentioned in Scripture, such as the judgment of the church (2 Cor. 5:10), the judgment of Israel, and the purging of the rebels as a prelude to the millennial kingdom (Ezek. 20:33–38). It is also different from the judgment of the wicked dead resurrected at the judgment of the great white throne (Rev. 20:11–15), which will occur at the end of the millennium.

The time of this judgment is clearly stated in Matthew 25:31: "When the Son of Man comes in his glory, and all the angels with him, he will sit on his glorious throne." The judgment is not of all people but of living Gentiles. The Gentiles are described as either sheep or goats, and Jews are described as brothers of Christ.

Taken as a whole, this judgment fits naturally into the premillennial order of events before and after the second coming of Christ. This judgment related to the Gentiles is similar to the judgment related to Israel (Ezek. 20:33–38). The contrast of Jews and Gentiles is a familiar one in Scripture as Gentiles are distinguished from the Jews in their outlook and hope (Rom. 11:13; 15:27; 16:4; Gal. 2:12). They are contrasted to those who are considered Jews as in Romans 3:29 and 9:24.

Matthew 25:31–46, however, has puzzled expositors because there is no preaching of the cross, there is no statement of the gospel as necessary for salvation, and all the passage speaks of is the contrast of the works of the sheep and the goats. The answer to this problem is not a denial that salvation is based on faith and grace alone (Rom. 3:10–12, 21, 28). The passage can be seen in the light of James 2:26, which declares, "Faith without deeds is dead." Presented here is not the grounds of salvation but the fruit of salvation.

The Olivet Discourse takes its place among the great prophetic passages of Scripture. The judgment explains why Christ did not bring His kingdom in at His first coming: Other prophecies had to be fulfilled before the second coming could be fulfilled. Accordingly, while Christ was declared the King of Israel and the Savior of the world, He was rejected at His first coming but will return in triumph, fulfilling literally the passage in the Old Testament that describes this victory.

The disciples were ill prepared to understand this, and they no doubt did not understand at the time as they asked the further question in Acts 1 concerning the time that Christ would bring in His kingdom. The early church was slow to respond and understand that there would be an extensive time period between the first coming of Christ and His second coming and that in it would be fulfilled God's program.

JESUS IS BRINGING HIS WHOLE ARMY AT THE SECOND COMING

> Enoch, the seventh from Adam, prophesied about them: "See, the Lord is coming with thousands upon thousands of his holy ones to judge everyone, and to convict all of them of all the ungodly acts they have committed in their ungodliness, and of all the defiant words ungodly sinners have spoken against him." (Jude vv. 14–15)

Jude quoted from Enoch who, like Elijah, went to heaven without experiencing death (Heb. 11:5). This prophecy concerning the second coming of Christ emphasized the fact that He will be accompanied by thousands of angels and, on that occasion, will judge the wickedness of ungodly people in keeping with Jude's previous statements concerning the extent of apostasy and God's judgment on them.

A similar truth is emphasized in Revelation 19:11–21, when Christ returns. As included here in Jude's epistle, there is a reminder that God will deal with those who teach false doctrine and who are apostate concerning the faith. Their hypocrisy, wickedness, and unbelief are described graphically in the preceding verses. The reader is warned against apostates and against following their teaching and at the same time is alerted to the fact that the apostates are subject to God's searching judgments.

CHRIST WILL DESTROY ALL WICKEDNESS AND SIN AT THE SECOND COMING

But the day of the Lord will come like a thief. The heavens will disappear with a roar; the elements will be destroyed by fire, and the earth and everything done in it will be laid bare.

Since everything will be destroyed in this way, what kind of people ought you to be? You ought to live holy and godly lives as you look forward to the day of God and speed its coming. That day will bring about the destruction of the heavens by fire, and the elements will melt in the heat. But in keeping with

his promise we are looking forward to a new heaven
and a new earth, where righteousness dwells.

So then, dear friends, since you are looking forward to this, make every effort to be found spotless,
blameless and at peace with him. (2 Pet. 3:10–14)

Earlier references to the day of the Lord, as in 1 Thessalonians 5,
described the period as beginning with the rapture and continuing
through the tribulation period and finishing at the end of the millennium. In 2 Peter 3, the whole picture is again revealed with emphasis
on the final end of it: "But the day of the Lord will come like a thief.
The heavens will disappear with a roar; the elements will be destroyed
by fire, and the earth and everything in it will be laid bare" (v. 10). This
will occur not at the beginning but at the end of the day of the Lord,
which will be the end of the millennial kingdom (Rev. 20:11; 21:1).
The description of the earth being destroyed by fire is catastrophic
and supports the conclusion that the new earth, created according
to Revelation 21:1, will entirely replace our present earth. As scien-
tists know, the earth is composed of atomic structure, which is held
together by the power of God. Just as God created it out of nothing,
so He can dismiss it into nothing in preparation for the eternal state.

Christ's second coming will kick off the millennial kingdom.
When that kingdom comes to an end, there will be a new heaven
and a new earth. God is not coming to repair His broken world but
to replace it with one that is perfect. Before this ultimate destruction
and rebirth, Christ will reign on earth for a thousand years, which we
will explore in the next chapter.

5

THE MILLENNIAL KINGDOM

What does Scripture mean when it talks about the millennium? What will this period of time look like? Will we know when it has begun—or has it already started? Many Christians disagree on this topic, but a careful study of the prophecies in Scripture can provide clear answers.

VARIOUS VIEWS OF THE MILLENNIUM

> They came to life and reigned with Christ a thousand years. (Rev. 20:4)

A major division in the theology of the church has concerned the question of whether there will be a thousand-year reign of Christ after His second coming. Both the postmillennial and the amillennial views hold that the fulfillment of the millennium is achieved before His second coming, with amillenarians more or less explaining away any literal fulfillment. As such, Revelation 20 should be studied carefully to see what its contribution is and whether it teaches a kingdom on earth of which Christ will be king.

The popular view among premillenarians is that the kingdom following the second coming of Christ is a fulfillment of God's theocratic program, in keeping with the promise given to David that his kingdom and throne would continue forever over Israel. Those who interpret the prophecies literally view Christ as reigning supremely over the entire world as a political leader, beginning with the second coming. This viewpoint is often called the dispensational point of view, but a preferable designation would be those who hold to a literal kingdom on earth. Basically, this view takes into consideration the fact that Christ fulfills in a literal way what was prophesied in the Scripture concerning the kingdom on earth.

The amillennial interpretation, which is probably the majority view of the church today, tends to minimize the promise of a kingdom on earth. Amillenarians are not all agreed as to how to arrive at this conclusion. Their viewpoint is called amillennial because their view is nonmillennial, that is, there will be no literal kingdom on earth with Christ reigning on the throne.

Some feel that the entire present age is the millennial kingdom and that God is reigning in the hearts of those who put their trust in Him. This, of course, does not provide any literal fulfillment of the millennial kingdom. Others hold that the millennial kingdom is being fulfilled in heaven through Christ's spiritual reign over the earth. Often they do not consider the period a literal thousand years, and they minimize the literal meaning of the prophecies relating to it.

Some amillenarians now hold that the millennium will be fulfilled in the new heaven and new earth in eternity and, therefore, does not need to be fulfilled now. The problem with all of these points of view is that they do not provide a cogent explanation of many passages in the Old Testament and in the New Testament that teach a literal kingdom.

THE BINDING OF SATAN

> And I saw an angel coming down out of heaven, having the key to the Abyss and holding in his hand a great chain. He seized the dragon, that ancient serpent, who is the devil, or Satan, and bound him for a thousand years. He threw him into the Abyss, and locked and sealed it over him, to keep him from deceiving the nations anymore until the thousand years were ended. After that, he must be set free for a short time. (Rev. 20:1–3)

In Revelation 20, John recorded what he saw concerning the binding of Satan. Inasmuch as the event's duration is a matter of direct divine revelation that John has told, the one thousand years must also be taken as a literal figure because God revealed it as so. If God were in any way to try to describe the literal binding of Satan and his being inactive for one thousand years, He could not have done it in any more graphic or clear way than He did in these three verses.

The events of verses 1–3 are clearly chronological in order and in total support of the premillennial interpretation. The passage makes clear that Satan is not simply restricted, as some would teach, but he is totally inactive in the millennium. By contrast, the New Testament teaches that Satan is still very much alive and well in the present age. In Acts 5:3, Ananias was declared to be filled with Satan and motivated by him in lying about his sale of property. In 2 Corinthians 4:3–4, the statement is made that Satan is active in blinding the eyes of those who hear the gospel so that they will not see it and understand it. According to Ephesians 2:2, the unsaved are working in the power of Satan. In 1 Thessalonians 2:18, Satan was revealed to have hindered Paul in his desire to come to the Thessalonians. The most decisive text is in 1 Peter 5:8: "Be alert and of sober mind. Your enemy the devil prowls around like a roaring lion looking for someone to devour."

Though Satan is somewhat restricted by God, as in the case of Job, these passages teach dramatically that he is not bound in the present age. Satan is active in the world and a leader in all its rebellion against God. Nevertheless, Christians can depend on God's protecting power, and the one thousand years will follow the second coming.

THE RESURRECTION OF THE TRIBULATION SAINTS

> I saw thrones on which were seated those who had been given authority to judge. And I saw the souls of those who had been beheaded because of their testimony about Jesus and because of the word of God. They had not worshiped the beast or its image and had not received its mark on their foreheads or their hands. They came to life and reigned with Christ a thousand years. (Rev. 20:4)

With Satan out of the way, the revelation now turns to what God will do for the saints in this period (Rev. 20:4–6). Those who had refused to worship the beast had been executed, and a great host of martyrs went to heaven during the time of the great tribulation. This had happened in the three and a half years preceding the second coming. They are described as "a great multitude" (7:9). Here they are resurrected and honored because they had not received the mark of the beast, and the purpose of the resurrection is that they would reign with Christ one thousand years. This is a clear support for a millennial kingdom following the second coming of Christ. The chronology is quite evident.

These martyred dead were killed in the period just before the second coming. Now Christ causes the saints who had been martyred in the tribulation to be resurrected in order to reign with Him for one thousand years. There is no way to avoid the implication that the millennium is subsequent to the second coming of Christ in this passage, as it is subsequent to the death and resurrection of the martyrs.

The question has been raised concerning those who are seated on the throne to judge (Rev. 20:4). Many scriptures contribute to the fact that saints will share in the reign of Christ. Jesus told His disciples, "And I confer on you a kingdom, just as my Father conferred one on me, so that you may eat and drink at my table in my kingdom and sit on thrones, judging the twelve tribes of Israel" (Luke 22:29–30).

Obviously, those who reign with Christ will not have equal status but will be subject to Christ and acting on His behalf. The millennial kingdom, however, is not discussed, except that it is clear that it will begin with the second coming of Christ and will end with judgment on the world and a creation of a new heaven and new earth.

MAJOR FEATURES OF THE MILLENNIUM

> He will not judge by what he sees with his eyes,
> or decide by what he hears with his ears;
> but with righteousness he will judge the needy,
> with justice he will give decisions for the poor
> of the earth.
> He will strike the earth with the rod of his mouth;
> with the breath of his lips he will slay the wicked.
> Righteousness will be his belt
> and faithfulness the sash around his waist.
> (Isa. 11:3–5)

The millennial kingdom is described at length in many biblical passages. Though the exact figure of one thousand years is not mentioned except in Revelation 20, the fact of a kingdom that has a long duration is clearly the intent of the prophetic passages (Isa. 2:2–4; 11:4–9; Ps. 72). According to the Old Testament, Jerusalem will be the capital of the millennial kingdom (Isa. 2:3). War will cease (v. 4). The millennial kingdom will be characterized by righteousness, peace, and tranquillity, and there will be justice for all the oppressed (11:3–5). Even the ferocity of beasts will be tamed (vv. 6–9). Isaiah summarized the thought in verse 9: "They will neither harm nor destroy on all my holy mountain, for the earth will be filled with the knowledge of the LORD as the waters cover the sea."

Psalm 72, as well as many other psalms, gives the glowing prophetic picture of the future millennium. The future is described as flourishing and the government as righteous, and abundant peace is promised as long as the moon endures. All kings bow down before Christ, and His rule extends from sea to sea. The earth will be filled with the glory of God. The desire of nations for peace, righteousness, knowledge of the Lord, economic justice, and deliverance from Satan will have its prophetic fulfillment. The major factors of the millennium, including Christ's absolute power, will include the perfect and righteous government and ideal circumstances on the earth. In many respects, the rule of Christ as the last Adam replaces what God had intended for Adam, who was placed in charge of the garden of Eden.

Many passages in the Old Testament emphasize the fact that Israel will have a prominent place. According to Ezekiel 20:33–38, at the time of the second coming Israel will experience a purging judgment and only the righteous, godly remnant will be allowed to enter the kingdom. Israel, pictured in the Old Testament as being an untrue wife, will now be rejoined to Christ in the symbol of marriage and experience the love of Christ (Hosea 2:14–23).

Though Israel will enjoy the blessings of being regathered to its ancient land and under the special rule of Christ, the rest of the world will also experience the rule of Christ as King of Kings. The nation of Israel, however, will also have the benefits of the rule of David resurrected from the dead as a regent of Christ (Jer. 30:9; Ezek. 34:23–24; 37:24–25).

THE MILLENNIAL KINGDOM ESTABLISHED

> The LORD will be king over the whole earth. On
> that day there will be one LORD, and his name the
> only name. (Zech. 14:9)

Zechariah 14:9–21 reveals that the millennial kingdom will be distinguished by the fact that Jesus Christ will rule over the entire earth. An indication of the rule of Christ as King of Kings is that He will judge the nations that fought against Jerusalem (vv. 12–13). A plague will seize man and beast alike, but a great quantity of gold, silver, and clothing will accrue to Israel's benefit (v. 14).

Those who survive the purging judgments at the beginning of the millennial kingdom will be required to worship Christ annually (v. 16). If they do not worship Him as commanded, God will hold their rain (vv. 17–19). It will be a time when the holiness of God is especially revealed, and false elements such as the Canaanites will be shut out (vv. 20–21). The partial revelation of the nature of the millennial kingdom as described here is amplified in many other scriptures in both the Old Testament and the New Testament.

THE GLORY OF THE KINGDOM

In that day the Branch of the LORD will be beautiful and glorious, and the fruit of the land will be the pride and glory of the survivors in Israel. Those who are left in Zion, who remain in Jerusalem, will be called holy, all who are recorded among the living in Jerusalem. The Lord will wash away the filth of the women of Zion; he will cleanse the bloodstains from Jerusalem by a spirit of judgment and a spirit of fire. Then the LORD will create over all of Mount Zion and over those who assemble there a cloud of smoke by day and a glow of flaming fire by night;

> over everything the glory will be a canopy. It will be
> a shelter and shade from the heat of the day, and a
> refuge and hiding place from the storm and rain.
> (Isa. 4:2–6)

The expression "in that day" sometimes refers to the contemporary scene, sometimes to the future millennium, as determined by the context. In Isaiah 4:2–6, the beauty of the millennial reign is described.

Isaiah predicted cleansing of the bloodstains of Jerusalem and the presence of the Lord over Mount Zion, signified by a cloud of smoke by day and fire by night (v. 5). In the millennial kingdom, the day will come when Israel will be cleansed from sin and its glory restored (Zeph. 3:14–20).

THE PSALMIST'S PICTURE OF THE MILLENNIUM

> A little while, and the wicked will be no more;
>   though you look for them, they will not be
>   found.
> But the meek will inherit the land
>   and enjoy peace and prosperity. (Ps. 37:10–11)

In Psalm 37, David declared his delight in the Lord and expressed his confidence that as people commit to the Lord, they will receive what their hearts desire (vv. 4–6). He spoke also of the future revelation of the righteousness and justice of his cause (v. 6).

David predicted judgment on the wicked and that the meek would inherit the land (vv. 9–11). He saw also that the wicked would perish in contrast to the Lord upholding the righteous (vv. 20–24). David expressed his faith that the Lord would protect His own and give them the land for an inheritance in contrast to the wicked, who would be cut off (vv. 27–29). This theme was continued in verses 34 and 37–38. This was fulfilled in history and will be fulfilled in the millennium (Amos 9:15).

THE FUTURE MESSIANIC KINGDOM

> In the last days
> the mountain of the LORD's temple will be
> established
> as the highest of the mountains;
> it will be exalted above the hills,
> and all nations will stream to it.
> Many peoples will come and say,
> "Come, let us go up to the mountain of the LORD,
> to the temple of the God of Jacob.
> He will teach us his ways,
> so that we may walk in his paths."
> (Isa. 2:2–3)

Isaiah 2 predicts the future kingdom of the Messiah. Jerusalem is described as the capital of the world in a time of peace rather than war, a time when the Lord will teach His ways (vv. 3–5). This will be fulfilled in the millennium.

THE COMING SON OF DAVID

> Nevertheless, there will be no more gloom for those
> who were in distress....
>
> The people walking in darkness
> > have seen a great light;
> on those living in the land of deep darkness
> > a light has dawned.
> You have enlarged the nation
> > and increased their joy;
> they rejoice before you
> > as people rejoice at the harvest,
> as warriors rejoice
> > when dividing the plunder. (Isa. 9:1–3)

In Isaiah 9, the coming of the Messiah is compared to a time when a great light will shine (v. 2) and a time of joy and rejoicing (v. 3). The time is pictured as a great victory of Israel (vv. 4–5).

The great prophecy of the coming of Christ is recorded in verses 6–7:

> For to us a child is born,
> > to us a son is given,
> > and the government will be on his shoulders.
> And he will be called
> > Wonderful Counselor, Mighty God,
> > Everlasting Father, Prince of Peace.

> Of the greatness of his government and peace
>   there will be no end.
> He will reign on David's throne
>   and over his kingdom,
> establishing and upholding it
>   with justice and righteousness
>   from that time on and forever.
> The zeal of the LORD Almighty
>   will accomplish this.

This passage is one of the great messianic prophecies of the Old Testament describing Christ as possessing the attributes of God. He will be "Everlasting Father," not in the sense of being God the Father, the first person of the Trinity, but in the sense that He will be like a father in His government over Israel in the millennial kingdom. The peace of that period is indicated in the title "Prince of Peace" (v. 6).

As God promised David, his kingdom would go on forever, being fulfilled by the millennial kingdom. God will continue to be sovereign over creation throughout eternity to come. The prophecy specified that His throne would be David's throne (v. 7), in fulfillment of the Davidic covenant indicating that this throne, like David's kingdom, would be on earth, not in heaven. This kingdom will be distinguished as one of justice and righteousness (Isa. 11:3–5). The kingdom will be realized by the power of God: "The zeal of the LORD Almighty will accomplish this" (9:7).

These prophecies, as interpreted in their normal literal sense, predict fulfillment of the expectation of a kingdom on earth after the second coming of Christ, in keeping with the premillennial interpretation of Scripture. In Isaiah 9, as in many passages in the Old Testament, the first and second comings of Christ are not distinguished, and the child who was born (v. 6) in Bethlehem in His first coming will be the same person described as the Everlasting King who will reign forever (v. 7). The theme of the future kingdom of Christ on earth is a familiar subject of the prophecies of Isaiah (11:4; 16:5; 28:5–6, 17; 32:16; 33:5; 42:1, 3–4; 51:5).

THE COMING GLORIOUS KINGDOM

> On this mountain the LORD Almighty will prepare
> a feast of rich food for all peoples,
> a banquet of aged wine—
> the best of meats and the finest of wines.
> On this mountain he will destroy
> the shroud that enfolds all peoples,
> the sheet that covers all nations;
> he will swallow up death forever.
> The Sovereign LORD will wipe away the tears
> from all faces. (Isa. 25:6–8)

Isaiah 25–26 predicts God's triumph and His people's praise of God for His omnipotent deliverance of His people. These prophecies to some extent have been fulfilled in the past but will have their ultimate and complete fulfillment in God's future millennial kingdom. In that future time, those who have trusted God will be honored and those who are God's enemies will be brought down (25:12).

LORD, you establish peace for us;
>   all that we have accomplished you have done
>   for us....

We have not brought salvation to the earth,
>   and the people of the world have not come to
>   life.

But your dead will live, LORD;
>   their bodies will rise—
let those who dwell in the dust
>   wake up and shout for joy—
your dew is like the dew of the morning.
>   (Isa. 26:12, 18–19)

This is another long psalm of praise recognizing the Lord's faithfulness in caring for His people. The future kingdom will be a time of peace (v. 12). It will also be a time of resurrection of the dead (vv. 18–19). The deliverance of the righteous in resurrection at the beginning of the millennium refers to the Old Testament saints (Dan. 12:1–2). Isaiah 26:19 and Daniel 12:1–2 reveal the most important prophecies of resurrection of the Old Testament saints.

PREPARING THE WAY FOR THE KING

[Jerusalem,] the nations will see your vindication,
>   and all kings your glory;
you will be called by a new name

that the mouth of the LORD will bestow.

You will be a crown of splendor in the LORD's
hand,

a royal diadem in the hand of your God.

(Isa. 62:2–3)

In Isaiah 62, another beautiful prophetic picture of the future kingdom is revealed as following the second coming of Christ. At that time Jerusalem's salvation will be evident to all (v. 1). The nations near Israel will observe her righteousness and glory (v. 2). Israel is compared to a crown or a royal diadem (v. 3). Though she once was described as desolate, now she will be called "Hephzibah," meaning "my delight is in her," and her land "Beulah," meaning "married one," for "the LORD will take delight in you, and your land will be married" (v. 4). Her restoration is described as a joyful marriage.

Israel will never have to surrender to foreigners her new wine or her crops (vv. 6–9). Israel was challenged to prepare the road for the King (vv. 10–11). The people of Israel themselves will be described as "the Holy People" (v. 12).

A KINGDOM OF PEACE AND JOY

But be glad and rejoice forever
in what I will create,
for I will create Jerusalem to be a delight
and its people a joy.
I will rejoice over Jerusalem
and take delight in my people;

> the sound of weeping and of crying
>> will be heard in it no more.
>
> Never again will there be in it
>> an infant who lives but a few days,
>> or an old man who does not live out his years;
> the one who dies at a hundred
>> will be thought a mere child. (Isa. 65:18–20)

Isaiah 65:17–25 presents a glorious picture of the ultimate new heaven and new earth. The passage then returns to the theme of Jerusalem in the millennial kingdom, in which there will be longevity but also death. One who dies at one hundred years will be considered still a youth. The millennial earth will provide Israel with security. "They will build houses and dwell in them; they will plant vineyards and eat their fruit" (v. 21). By contrast, the wicked will not take possessions away from the people of Israel: "My chosen ones will long enjoy the work of their hands" (v. 22). Israel's children will not be "doomed to misfortune" (v. 23). Tranquillity in nature will also occur: "The wolf and the lamb will feed together, and the lion will eat straw like the ox, and dust will be the serpent's food. They will neither harm nor destroy on all my holy mountain" (v. 25; see also 11:6–7). These prophecies do not fit the eternal New Jerusalem but relate to the millennium.

In expressing Israel's future hope, the Old Testament often mingles prophecies of the millennial kingdom with that of the New Jerusalem in eternity. The distinctions are made clear when the details are observed. Here, obviously, the millennial kingdom is being described, because in the New Jerusalem there will be no death, no sin, and no judgment. The millennial kingdom will be a time of great joy and rejoicing and deliverance for the people of God, but death and sin will still be present.

THE HOPE OF RIGHTEOUSNESS IN THE MILLENNIAL KINGDOM

> For this is what the LORD says:
>
> "I will extend peace to her like a river,
>   and the wealth of nations like a flooding
>   stream;
> you will nurse and be carried on her arm
>   and dandled on her knees.
> As a mother comforts her child,
>   so will I comfort you;
>   and you will be comforted over Jerusalem."
>   (Isa. 66:12–13)

Isaiah 66 describes the millennial kingdom following the second coming of Christ. Because heaven is God's throne, it follows that earth is His "footstool" (v. 1). Accordingly, no temple can really contain Him. God declared that Israel's sacrifices would be of no use unless her heart was with Him. He promised to judge with justice those who were not living in right relationship with Him (vv. 2–6).

Israel's restoration will be like a child born before its time. Israel will be delivered and restored quickly (vv. 7–9). God commanded her to rejoice (v. 10). In the future millennium, God also promised to care for His people like a mother cares for her baby (vv. 11–13). Israel "will flourish like grass" (v. 14). But the wicked will see God descending on them in judgment (vv. 15–17). Even the nations will come to see the glory of God, and those not of the nation of Israel will be brought to Jerusalem to worship God (vv. 19–21).

The final verses of Isaiah repeat the promise that God will care for His own forever, in contrast to those who experience eternal punishment (vv. 22–24). The close of the book of Isaiah is a stern warning to those who reject God and a word of assurance to those who put their trust in Him. These prophecies will be fulfilled in the millennium.

THE ROCK OF THE MILLENNIAL KINGDOM

> While you were watching, a rock was cut out, but not by human hands. It struck the statue on its feet of iron and clay and smashed them. Then the iron, the clay, the bronze, the silver and the gold were all broken to pieces and became like chaff on a threshing floor in the summer. The wind swept them away without leaving a trace. But the rock that struck the statue became a huge mountain and filled the whole earth.…
>
> In the time of those kings, the God of heaven will set up a kingdom that will never be destroyed, nor will it be left to another people. It will crush all those kingdoms and bring them to an end, but it will itself endure forever. This is the meaning of the vision of the rock cut out of a mountain, but not

by human hands—a rock that broke the iron, the
bronze, the clay, the silver and the gold to pieces.

The great God has shown the king what will take
place in the future. The dream is true and its interpretation is trustworthy. (Dan. 2:34–35, 44–45)

Daniel recorded a strangely specific dream of the pagan king
Nebuchadnezzar. The kingdom represented by the rock is the kingdom that Christ will inaugurate at His second coming. It will destroy
all previous kingdoms.

Daniel summarized the whole vision as God showing the king
what will take place in the future (v. 45). This prophetic revelation
makes clear that the kingdom from heaven is not a spiritual kingdom,
which by spiritual processes would gradually conquer the earth, but
rather a sudden catastrophic judgment from heaven destroying the
political kingdoms of the Gentiles. This will pave the way for a political millennial kingdom that will begin with the second coming of
Christ. The destruction of the Gentile world powers is an event, not
a process, and will be fulfilled by Christ in the second coming.

CHRIST'S AUTHORITY IN THE MILLENNIAL KINGDOM

In my vision at night I looked, and there before me
was one like a son of man, coming with the clouds
of heaven. He approached the Ancient of Days and
was led into his presence. He was given authority,
glory and sovereign power; all nations and peoples

> of every language worshiped him. His dominion
> is an everlasting dominion that will not pass away,
> and his kingdom is one that will never be destroyed.
> (Dan. 7:13–14)

The coming of the "son of man" (v. 13) could be understood as referring to the coming of Jesus Christ as the Messiah in His second coming, as Christ Himself used the expression "the Son of Man" in many references to Himself in the New Testament (e.g., Matt. 8:20; 9:6; 10:23; 11:19; 12:8, 32, 40).

Daniel 7:13 refers to Jesus Christ in His incarnation approaching "the Ancient of Days," an obvious reference to God the Father. The reference to giving Him complete authority over all peoples will be fulfilled in His millennial kingdom, which, as far as dominion is concerned, will continue forever (v. 14).

THE FUTURE GLORIOUS KINGDOM

> In the last days
> the mountain of the LORD's temple will be
> established
> as the highest of the mountains;
> it will be exalted above the hills,
> and peoples will stream to it. (Mic. 4:1)

Micah 4 describes the glorious future kingdom. The first three verses are almost identical to Isaiah 2:2–4. The glorious temple is said to be established "in the last days." This has its fulfillment in the millennium when Ezekiel's temple (Ezek. 40–44) will be built. As far as Micah's foresight was concerned, the temple could have been established soon, as he did not contemplate the intervention of the present age of the church. People from all over the world will come to visit the Lord's temple.

Even the Gentiles will seek to come to the temple. They will say, "He will teach us his ways, so that we may walk in his paths" (Mic. 4:2). Zion and Jerusalem will be the center from which the law goes forth. The contemporary situation in the kingdom will be one of peace because "they will beat their swords into plowshares and their spears into pruning hooks. Nation will not take up sword against nation, nor will they train for war anymore" (v. 3). The people will be at peace, and "everyone will sit under their own vine and under their own fig tree, and no one will make them afraid, for the LORD Almighty has spoken" (v. 4). In this kingdom period the Lord will rule them in Mount Zion and will restore the governmental dominion of Zion. These prophecies will be fulfilled in the millennial kingdom.

> The remnant of Jacob will be among the nations,
>> in the midst of many peoples,
> like a lion among the beasts of the forest,
>> like a young lion among flocks of sheep,
> which mauls and mangles as it goes,
>> and no one can rescue.
> Your hand will be lifted up in triumph over your
>> enemies,
>> and all your foes will be destroyed. (Mic. 5:8–9)

In Micah 5, we see that although Assyria would invade Israel's land and conquer her for a time, ultimately the people of Israel will prevail and be like a lion among the beasts of the forests (vv. 5–8). Micah predicted, "Your hand will be lifted up in triumph over your enemies, and all your foes will be destroyed" (v. 9). When that day comes, God will bring about the destruction of that which is evil in the midst of Israel: their chariots, their witchcraft, their carved images, and their Asherah poles (vv. 10–14). God's vengeance will be against Israel as well as the nations (v. 15). This prophecy will be fulfilled in the millennial kingdom.

THE FINAL REBELLION AGAINST CHRIST

> When the thousand years are over, Satan will be released from his prison and will go out to deceive the nations in the four corners of the earth—Gog and Magog—and to gather them for battle. In number they are like the sand on the seashore. They marched across the breadth of the earth and surrounded the camp of God's people, the city he loves. But fire came down from heaven and devoured them. And the devil, who deceived them, was thrown into the lake of burning sulfur, where the beast and the false prophet had been thrown. They will be tormented day and night for ever and ever. (Rev. 20:7–10)

John described the climax of the millennial kingdom as one last battle against Satan. Satan and his attackers come from all nations of the world. They gather about the city of Jerusalem in attempting to capture the capital city, but fire comes down from heaven and devours them. There will be no earthly aftermath to this battle at the end of the millennium. Life does not go on after this battle, for the world immediately moves into the new heaven and new earth situation.

People have asked the question why Satan would be loosed from his prison after one thousand years. This action is in keeping with God's purpose to demonstrate in history that people left to their own devices will sin against God. Even though the millennium provides a perfect environment for humanity with abundant revelation of God's power, the evil heart of man is manifest in the fact that people reject Christ and follow Satan when he is loosed. The releasing of Satan also is a demonstration of the wickedness of Satan and the fallen angels and how even one thousand years in confinement does not change this.

The important thing to keep in mind when studying the issues surrounding the end times is this: Faithful believers will be invited to experience the glory and communion of God's everlasting kingdom. The details of these prophecies are worth careful study, but they should never supplant our trust in God's character. He alone is mighty and just, and He will be faithful to save.

6

GOD'S CHOSEN PEOPLE: ISRAEL IN PROPHECY

When Christ came to earth, He came with a mission to redeem all people: first the Jews and then the Gentiles. Sadly, the nation of Israel rejected its Messiah, as the prophet Isaiah had predicted. However, Israel is still a part of God's plan; His love for Israel is everlasting, and His covenant remains. The nation will be restored during the millennial kingdom, as explained in the many prophecies in this chapter.

ISRAEL'S ULTIMATE RESTORATION

> Then the eyes of those who see will no longer be
> closed,
> and the ears of those who hear will listen.
> (Isa. 32:3)

Isaiah 32 teaches that Israel will have "a king" who "will reign in righteousness and rulers will rule with justice" (v. 1). Isaiah predicted that Israel at that time would listen to God's exhortation (vv. 2–8). God promised Israel severe judgment but also ultimate restoration and deliverance (vv. 9–20). The passage concludes, "How blessed you will be, sowing your seed by every stream, and letting your cattle and donkeys range free" (v. 20). This will be fulfilled in the millennium (Jer. 23:5–8; Rev. 19:11–15).

ISRAEL'S ULTIMATE DELIVERANCE

> Look on Zion, the city of our festivals;
>> your eyes will see Jerusalem,
>> a peaceful abode, a tent that will not be moved;
> its stakes will never be pulled up,
>> nor any of its ropes broken.
> There the LORD will be our Mighty One.
>> (Isa. 33:20–21)

In Isaiah 33, future judgment was pronounced on Israel. This would be followed, however, by Israel's restoration (vv. 5–6). The judgment of God on those who disobey Him, however, was described in graphic terms (vv. 7–14). By contrast, those who were righteous will be blessed of the Lord (vv. 15–18). They "will see the king in his beauty and view a land that stretches afar" (v. 17). The future restoration of Israel and the deliverance of the people of Israel were predicted by Isaiah (vv. 20–24). This will be ultimately fulfilled in the millennium.

ISRAEL TO BE RESTORED

> For I am the LORD your God,
>> the Holy One of Israel, your Savior....

> Since you are precious and honored in my sight,
> and because I love you,
> I will give people in exchange for you,
> nations in exchange for your life. (Isa. 43:3–4)

Isaiah 43 shows that God, who created Israel, would be with the nation through the deep waters as well as the fires of her affliction (vv. 1–2). The ultimate purpose of God is to bring the people of Israel back to the Holy Land from being scattered all over the world (vv. 3–7). This has been fulfilled only partially in return from the captivities and awaits its complete fulfillment at the second coming of Christ (Ezek. 39:26–28). In supernaturally restoring Israel, God will make the nation a testimony to His own deity and power (Isa. 43:8–13).

In the immediate future, God would deliver Israel from Babylon (vv. 14–21). But in spite of God's goodness, Israel would not respond (vv. 22–24). God reminded her that only He would be able to blot out her transgressions or punish her for her sins (vv. 25–28). This prophecy will be fulfilled in the millennial kingdom.

GOD WILL FULFILL HIS PROMISES TO ISRAEL

> The LORD will surely comfort Zion
> and will look with compassion on all her ruins;
> he will make her deserts like Eden,
> her wastelands like the garden of the LORD.
> Joy and gladness will be found in her,
> thanksgiving and the sound of singing.
>
> (Isa. 51:3)

In Isaiah 51, Israel was exhorted to look to Abraham and Sarah for examples of righteousness and to the Lord as the One who would fulfill the promises of blessing. The description of the situation corresponds to the millennial kingdom, when there will be universal joy and righteousness (vv. 3–5). God's salvation will last forever (v. 6). God was extolled as the One who would be able to bring the ransomed back to Zion (v. 11). God, who is her creator, will comfort Israel (v. 12). His power is greater than the power of Israel's oppressor (vv. 12–15). The cup of God's wrath drunk by Israel will be given to her oppressor (vv. 17–23). This prophecy will be completely fulfilled in the millennial kingdom.

GOD'S ULTIMATE PURPOSE TO RESTORE ISRAEL

> "However, the days are coming," declares the LORD, "when it will no longer be said, 'As surely as the LORD lives, who brought the Israelites up out of Egypt,' but it will be said, 'As surely as the LORD lives, who brought the Israelites up out of the land of the north and out of all the countries where he had banished them.' For I will restore them to the land I gave their ancestors." (Jer. 16:14–15)

Jeremiah 16:14–15 shows that although the near prospect for Israel was that of disaster and removal from the land, God affirmed that even in this context of apostasy He would restore them to the land.

Two things may be noted about this prophecy: (1) It was delivered in a time of apostasy when Israel certainly did not deserve this promise. (2) The promise of the land was still understood as a literal promise, as it is all through the Old Testament. Just as Israel was being literally carried off into captivity from her land to another, so she will be literally brought back from other lands to her homeland. The time of fulfillment will be at the second coming of Christ when Israelites will come "out of all the countries where he had banished them" (v. 15). Her regathering will enable her to participate in the millennial kingdom following the second advent.

THE RESTORATION OF ISRAEL TO HER LAND

> "The days are coming," declares the LORD, "when
> I will bring my people Israel and Judah back from
> captivity and restore them to the land I gave their
> ancestors to possess." (Jer. 30:3)

Jeremiah 30:1–11 is a far-reaching prophecy concerning the ultimate regathering of Israel and restoration to her land (vv. 2–3). In particular, the Lord prophesied a time of distress for Israel such as she had never experienced before (vv. 4–7; see also Matt. 24:15–30). However, God assured Israel that "he [Jacob] will be saved out of it" (Jer. 30:7).

God further predicted that Israel's slavery would end, and instead of serving foreigners, she would serve God and David her king (vv. 8–9). The timing of this prophecy is of great significance because it is linked to the resurrection of "David their king, whom I will raise up for them" (v. 9). David's resurrection will be connected with the second coming of Christ and will be part of the resurrection of Old Testament saints that will also occur at the time of the second coming (see Dan. 12:2–3). This prophecy has never been fulfilled and was part of the revelation contained in many Old Testament passages concerning the restoration of Israel to her land. This prophecy shows that Israel must undergo an unprecedented time of trouble before the second advent, will be rescued by Christ at His coming (coinciding with David's resurrection), and will enjoy deliverance and blessing in the time period following the second coming.

THE LATER RESTORATION OF ISRAEL

"Do not be afraid, Jacob my servant,
    for I am with you," declares the LORD.
"Though I completely destroy all the nations
    among which I scatter you,
    I will not completely destroy you.
I will discipline you but only in due measure;
    I will not let you go entirely unpunished."
                (Jer. 46:28)

In contrast to the destruction brought on Egypt, God reassured Israel that she would eventually be restored to her land and made safe and secure (Jer. 46:27). Though God would deal severely with those Israelites who fled to Egypt, ultimately the nation would be restored. God declared, "Though I completely destroy all the nations among which I scatter you, I will not completely destroy you. I will discipline you but only in due measure; I will not let you go entirely unpunished" (v. 28). This same thought was declared in Jeremiah 30:11. This was fulfilled in history and will be fulfilled in the millennium.

THE SIGN OF THE DRY BONES

> Then he said to me: "Son of man, these bones are the people of Israel. They say, 'Our bones are dried up and our hope is gone; we are cut off.' Therefore prophesy and say to them: 'This is what the Sovereign LORD says: My people, I am going to open your graves and bring you up from them; I will bring you back to the land of Israel. Then you, my people, will know that I am the LORD, when I open your graves and bring you up from them. I will put my Spirit in you and you will live, and I will settle you in your own land.'" (Ezek. 37:11–14)

In Ezekiel 37:1–14, the prophet was given a vision of a valley filled with dry bones. Ezekiel then was instructed to prophesy that these dry bones would come to life, that the bones would come together, that flesh would cover them, and finally that they would have the breath of life much like Adam (Gen. 2:7).

When Ezekiel obeyed the Lord and prophesied, "breath entered them [the bones]; they came to life and stood up on their feet—a vast army" (Ezek. 37:10).

Having given Ezekiel the vision, the Lord now interpreted it for him. In the interpretation, Ezekiel was informed that the bones represented Israel. Her hopeless, dried condition illustrated her hopelessness of ever being restored. In response to this, God promised to bring her back from death and to the land of Israel. God would put His Holy Spirit in her, and she would be settled in her own land.

In biblical interpretation today, many affirm that Israel will never be restored. They share the hopelessness that gripped the Israelites as they were scattered from their land to Assyria and Babylon. Contradicting this hopeless situation, God promised to restore Israel and in the strongest possible terms indicated that He would bring new life to her. He promised she would be restored as a nation, she would be indwelt by the Holy Spirit, and she would settle in her own land in safety.

The prediction that she would be brought up from the grave is partly symbolic in that the nation seemed to be dead and will be restored to physical life. But it is also to be considered literally, because according to Daniel 12:1–3, at the close of the great tribulation when Christ returns in His second coming, there will be a resurrection of Old Testament saints. Both figuratively and literally Israel will be restored and given new life. Those who have died and who were saved will be resurrected to share in the millennial kingdom as resurrected saints.

The promise that His Holy Spirit would be in Israel goes beyond her experience under the law, when the Holy Spirit was with her but not necessarily in her (John 14:17). Beginning on the day of Pentecost (Acts 2), all genuinely saved people are indwelt by the Holy Spirit, a situation that will continue until the rapture of the church.

Though there is no clear revelation of what will be true between the rapture and the second coming, Ezekiel 37:1–14 and other scriptures make it clear that the Holy Spirit will indwell the saints in the millennial kingdom (see Jer. 31:33).

THE SIGN OF THE TWO STICKS

> The word of the LORD came to me: "Son of man, take a stick of wood and write on it, 'Belonging to Judah and the Israelites associated with him.' Then take another stick of wood, and write on it, 'Belonging to Joseph (that is, to Ephraim) and all the Israelites associated with him.' Join them together into one stick so that they will become one in your hand." (Ezek. 37:15–17)

The situation being addressed in this prophecy was that of the divided kingdom. After Solomon, the ten tribes following Jeroboam became the kingdom of Israel; the two remaining tribes in Jerusalem, Judah and Benjamin, became the kingdom of Judah. The ten tribes were carried off to Assyria in 722 BC, and the two remaining tribes were carried off by Babylon between 605 and 586 BC. The situation in which these two kingdoms were divided will end, and as this and other prophecies predict, the two kingdoms will become one nation (Jer. 3:18; 23:5–6; 30:3; Hosea 1:11; Amos 9:11). No fulfillment has ever been recorded in history, and the future regathering of Israel will occur in the millennium.

GOD'S PROMISED RESTORATION OF ISRAEL

> I will now restore the fortunes of Jacob [or bring
> Jacob back from captivity] and will have compas-
> sion on all the people of Israel, and I will be zealous
> for my holy name. They will forget their shame and
> all the unfaithfulness they showed toward me when
> they lived in safety in their land with no one to
> make them afraid. (Ezek. 39:25–26)

In Ezekiel 39:25–29, God announced the restoration of Israel
as was predicted in many other passages in the Old Testament. God,
having previously predicted His judgments on Israel, here made a
special point of how the people of Israel will be gathered completely
from the various foreign lands to which they were scattered. This
was described in Ezekiel 38. In chapter 39, God made a specific and
sweeping prediction:

> When I have brought them back from the nations
> and have gathered them from the countries of their
> enemies, I will be proved holy through them in the
> sight of many nations. Then they will know that
> I am the LORD their God, for though I sent them
> into exile among the nations, I will gather them
> to their own land, not leaving any behind. I will
> no longer hide my face from them, for I will pour
> out my Spirit on the people of Israel, declares the
> Sovereign LORD. (vv. 27–29)

Not only will God restore Israel to the land, but He also promised to gather all of His people from their scattered positions and bring them back to the land. This will occur in the opening period of the millennial kingdom. It will not be an option to the children of Israel, but they will be commanded to come to their Promised Land. This is a dramatic prediction, and it supports the doctrine of a glorious future for Israel in the millennium.

Earlier in Ezekiel 20:33–38, God had declared His purpose to regather Israel but to purge the rebels or the unsaved so that only righteous Israel would be allowed to possess her ancient land. An important point in biblical interpretation is to treat these prophecies in the literal sense, as with the other prophecies that have been fulfilled. If so, it requires the second coming of Christ to occur before the thousand-year reign of Christ or the premillennial return of the Lord.

ISRAEL'S CYCLES OF JUDGMENT AND RESTORATION

"In that day I will respond,"
    declares the LORD …
"I will plant her for myself in the land;
    I will show my love to the one I called 'Not
        my loved one.'
I will say to those called 'Not my people,' 'You are
        my people';
    and they will say, 'You are my God.'"
        (Hosea 2:21, 23)

Hosea's cycle of judgment on sin and ultimate restoration began with a rebuke of Gomer as representing Israel (Hosea 1–2). It was predicted that she would be stripped naked, made like a desert without water, and disgraced (2:2–6). Her lovers would leave her, but God declared He would judge her and punish her (vv. 7–13). After the time of judgment, however, she would be restored to her husband (vv. 14–20). At that time she would be planted in the land (v. 23) and be loved by her husband; God would declare her "my people," and He would become her God (v. 23).

In keeping with this prophecy, Hosea was ordered by the Lord to reclaim his wife as he would buy a slave (3:1–3). She was to stay at home and not continue her adulterous life (v. 3).

The prophetic significance of this was stated: "For the Israelites will live many days without king or prince, without sacrifice or sacred stones, without ephod or household gods. Afterward the Israelites will return and seek the LORD their God and David their king. They will come trembling to the LORD and to his blessings in the last days" (3:4–5). This will be fulfilled at the second coming.

> For I will be like a lion to Ephraim,
>> like a great lion to Judah.
> I will tear them to pieces and go away;
>> I will carry them off, with no one to rescue them.
> Then I will return to my lair
>> until they have borne their guilt
>> and seek my face—
> in their misery
>> they will earnestly seek me. (Hosea 5:14–15)

In Hosea 4:1–6:3, the next cycle of judgment followed by restoration began with judgment on Israel: "No faithfulness, no love, no acknowledgment of God in the land.... Only cursing, lying and murder, stealing and adultery ... bloodshed follows bloodshed" (4:1–2). God predicted that though priests would increase in number, they would sin against God (v. 7). The people of Israel would be like them: "They will eat but not have enough; they will engage in prostitution but not flourish" (v. 10). They would make offerings to idols and engage in spiritual prostitution (vv. 11–14).

The indictment continued with charges of Israel's rebellion, corruption, and arrogance (5:1–5). Because of her sins, Israel would "be laid waste on the day of reckoning" (v. 9). Judgment was pronounced on "Ephraim," which represented the ten tribes of Israel. God predicted that the tribes would be carried off as captives (v. 14).

Though Israel was unrepentant, God promised that the day would come when they will "seek my face—in their misery they will earnestly seek me" (v. 15). God promised to restore them like the rain restores the earth (6:1–3). Ultimate restoration will be fulfilled at the second coming.

In Hosea 6:4–11:11, the prophet related another cycle of judgment and restoration that began with a series of indictments. God charged them, "Your love is like the morning mist, like the early dew that disappears. Therefore I cut you in pieces with my prophets, I killed you with the words of my mouth—then my judgments go forth like the sun" (6:4–5). His people were guilty of being unfaithful (v. 7); they "murder on the road to Shechem, carrying out their wicked schemes" (v. 9).

The indictment continued that Israel's sins were engulfing her (7:2), and she was like "all adulterers, burning like an oven whose fire the baker need not stir from the kneading of the dough till it rises" (v. 4). She was filled with passion (v. 6), and Ephraim was declared to be "a flat loaf not turned over" (v. 8). Ephraim was compared to a dove calling to Egypt and then to Assyria, both of whom would betray Israel (v. 11). The people gathered to drink wine but turned away from God (v. 14). They had broken their covenant with God (8:1) and had "rejected what is good" (v. 3). They worshipped a calf instead of the true God (vv. 4–6).

God was going to come on Israel like a whirlwind (v. 7), and she would become "something no one wants" (v. 8). Her altars would become places only for sinning (vv. 11–13). Because Israel had forgotten her God and Judah had attempted to fortify her cities, God would consume both with fire.

God predicted that His people would not remain in the land of Israel (9:3) but would go to Egypt, where they would be destroyed and their treasures taken away (vv. 3–6). God predicted the time of Israel's punishment was coming (v. 7), and He would punish her for her wickedness (vv. 7–9). She would be bereaved of her children (v. 12) and would be like a plant "blighted, their root is withered, they yield no fruit" (v. 16). As she started to become conscious of the wrath of God, she would "say to the mountains, 'Cover us!' and to the hills, 'Fall on us!'" (10:8).

God pleaded with her to return, but Israel was determined to turn away from Him. God promised, however, to bring about her ultimate restoration: "How can I give you up, Ephraim? How can I hand you over, Israel? How can I treat you like Admah? How can I make you like Zeboyim?" (11:8). God declared that His compassion was roused and that ultimately the children of Israel would come back to their land and be settled in their homes. This will be fulfilled at the second coming.

Though God's judgment was clearly pronounced on Israel and her sins had already been judged in history by events such as the Assyrian captivity and later the Babylonian captivity, the prophets were clear that there will come a time for ultimate restoration of Israel. While some of this was partially accomplished when the people came back from the Babylonian captivity, the ultimate fulfillment will be when the Lord returns, David is resurrected, and Israel is regathered permanently to her own land.

JOEL'S VISION OF ISRAEL'S FUTURE RESTORATION

> Judah will be inhabited forever
>   and Jerusalem through all generations.
>   (Joel 3:20)

In Joel 3, the prophet called for the armies of the nations to be roused and to assemble themselves for war in the Valley of Jehoshaphat, where they would encounter the judgment of God. Joel declared that God "will sit to judge all the nations on every side" (v. 12). On the basis of these prophecies being fulfilled, Joel pleaded with the multitudes to recognize that the day of the Lord was near (v. 14) and that it would be preceded by the darkening of the sun and the moon and the blotting out of the stars (v. 15). Ultimate fulfillment will be at the second coming.

In the preceding portion of the prophecy of Joel, God was declared to turn from Zion and be a refuge for His people. After the second coming, God will judge the wicked but will redeem His people Israel (Joel 3:16–21). Abundance of food, wine, and water will characterize the period for Israel in contrast to Egypt and Edom, which were described as desert wastes (vv. 18–19). When this restoration of Israel takes place, "Judah will be inhabited forever and Jerusalem through all generations" (v. 20). The prophet closed with a declaration that God will pardon Israel for her sins (v. 21). The prophecies of Joel are in harmony with the premillennial interpretation of Scripture because these events will take place before and after the second coming of Christ when Christ takes over as King of Kings and Lord of Lords.

AMOS'S VISION OF ISRAEL'S FUTURE RESTORATION

> I will plant Israel in their own land,
>   never again to be uprooted
>   from the land I have given them. (Amos 9:15)

After the recital of the many sins of Israel and God's certain judgment on them, Amos 9:11–15 describes the ultimate restoration of Israel, which will follow the times of God's judgment. The prophecies of Israel's complete restoration have never been fulfilled. Amos declared, however, "In that day I will restore David's fallen shelter—I will repair its broken walls and restore its ruins—and will rebuild it as it used to be" (v. 11). This promise was made in reference to the restoration of the Davidic kingdom, during which David will be resurrected from the dead to reign as king under Christ in the future kingdom, following the second coming (Jer. 30:9; Ezek. 34:23–24; 37:24). God promised that Israel will "possess the remnant of Edom" (Amos 9:12).

A time of prosperity was described for the kingdom: "when the reaper will be overtaken by the plowman and the planter by the one treading grapes" (v. 13).

God promised to "bring my people Israel back from exile. They will rebuild the ruined cities and live in them. They will plant vineyards and drink their wine; they will make gardens and eat their fruit" (v. 14). While this was fulfilled partially in the restoration of the people of Israel in the fourth and fifth centuries BC, its ultimate fulfillment will be related to the coming of Christ and Israel's permanent restoration.

The certainty of Israel's restoration—her being regathered to her land and again being blessed by the Lord—was summarized in Amos 9:15. This prophecy has obviously not been fulfilled, as Israel was scattered after AD 70 and Jerusalem was destroyed. This process of returning to the land is in stages. In the twentieth century the first stage, a partial restoration, has been fulfilled with the first of Israel returning to her land, beginning the process of her ultimate complete restoration. A second stage will be fulfilled after the covenant is signed with the Middle East ruler. The third stage will be fulfilled when Israel goes through her period of trouble in the great tribulation. The final stage will occur when she will be rescued at the second coming of Christ, and the prophecies of verses 11–15 will be fulfilled completely.

Because Israel has already returned to the land and formed a capital state, the biggest return since the time of Moses, the events of the last century seem to anticipate that God will fulfill the other aspects of Israel's restoration, which many believe will follow the rapture of the church. The prophet Amos, on the one hand, approved the righteousness of God by His judgment on the people of Israel and, on the other hand, manifested the grace of God, who will restore Israel to her land in fulfillment of His ultimate promises to Abraham and his descendants. Once restored, Israel will never be scattered again.

ISRAEL RESTORED THROUGH GOD'S GRACE

> Who is a God like you,
>> who pardons sin and forgives the
>>> transgression
>>> of the remnant of his inheritance?
> You do not stay angry forever
>> but delight to show mercy.
> You will again have compassion on us;
>> you will tread our sins underfoot
>> and hurl all our iniquities into the depths of
>>> the sea.
> You will be faithful to Jacob,
>> and show love to Abraham,
> as you pledged on oath to our ancestors
>> in days long ago. (Mic. 7:18–20)

In Micah 7, the prophet called attention to the departure of Israel from the laws of God. He declared, "The faithful have been swept from the land; not one upright person remains. Everyone lies in wait to shed blood; they hunt each other with nets" (v. 2).

He described Israel's hands as being "skilled in doing evil" (v. 3). Because of this, God was going to bring a time of confusion (v. 4).

By contrast, Micah, instead of seeking evil, looked for hope and waited for his Savior with confidence that God would hear him: "But as for me, I watch in hope for the LORD, I wait for God my Savior; my God will hear me" (v. 7).

Though it is true that Israel has sinned and will bear the wrath of God, the day will come when Israel will continue to build her walls and extend her boundaries. God's judgment on that day will be on the nations instead of on Israel.

In Israel's future, God will once again show her His miraculous wonders, and the world will see and be ashamed. The world will turn in fear to God. Micah asked rhetorically, "Who is a God like you, who pardons sin?" (v. 18). The future restoration of Israel will be based on the doctrine of grace rather than on the doctrine of judgment and will fulfill the covenant with Abraham, which God has pledged Himself to fulfill regardless of Israel's sins and shortcomings.

The mingled picture of prophecy, including Israel's condemnation and then glorification, is in keeping with the other scriptures describing this process in which Israel will ultimately be regathered and blessed by God in the millennial kingdom.

GOD WILL RESTORE ISRAEL

> On that day you, Jerusalem, will not be put to
> shame
> for all the wrongs you have done to me,
> because I will remove from you
> your arrogant boasters.
> Never again will you be haughty
> on my holy hill.
> But I will leave within you
> the meek and humble.
> The remnant of Israel
> will trust in the name of the LORD.
> They will do no wrong;
> they will tell no lies.
> A deceitful tongue
> will not be found in their mouths.
> They will eat and lie down
> and no one will make them afraid.
> (Zeph. 3:11–13)

Most important to God will be the restoration of the people of Israel in the day of the Lord. In Zephaniah 3, God declared that He would make Israel righteous again. This will be fulfilled in the millennium.

Though some spiritual revival took place in Israel when they returned from the Babylonian captivity to Jerusalem, the ultimate fulfillment will be in the millennial kingdom, following the second coming of Christ. Then there will be a true purging of that which is contrary to God and the nation of Israel, and those who are left will be the true worshippers.

THE REGATHERING OF ISRAEL

> Though I scatter them among the peoples,
>   yet in distant lands they will remember me.
> They and their children will survive,
>   and they will return. (Zech. 10:9)

In addition to any blessing that will come to Israel before the kingdom on earth, though God will scatter them in distant lands, His people will survive and come back from Egypt, Assyria, and other parts of the world (Zech. 10:9–10). When they pass through the "sea of trouble," they will be strengthened in contrast to God's judgment on Assyria and Egypt (vv. 11–12). This is one of many prophecies yet to be fulfilled that pictures Israel's being scattered over the world but regathered at the time of the second coming of Christ in order to possess their Promised Land.

GOD WILL RESTORE ISRAEL IN SPITE OF HER REJECTION OF THE MESSIAH

> Woe to the worthless shepherd,
>   who deserts the flock!
> May the sword strike his arm and his right eye!
>   May his arm be completely withered,
>   his right eye totally blinded! (Zech. 11:17)

Though scriptures had anticipated the ultimate restoration of Israel, the long process before this was fulfilled was related to their rejection of their Messiah. Accordingly, as written in Zechariah 11, the cedars of Lebanon, the oaks of Bashan, and the rich pastures of the land were all to be destroyed (vv. 1–3).

Zechariah shared a parable of a shepherd's relationship to a stubborn and rebellious flock. After a symbolic breaking of staves, Zechariah was then told to take the role of a foolish shepherd (v. 15), representing prophetically the Antichrist, who will lead Israel in the end time, and the false leader of Israel. Woe was pronounced on this restless shepherd (v. 17).

While all the prophetic details of this chapter are not clear, it generally indicates the reason why Israel's restoration did not take place sooner and points to her rejection of the Messiah in His first coming.

Despite Israel's rejection of the Messiah at His first coming, it was God's settled purpose to enthrone Christ as the King of Israel. The statement of this purpose of God was set in the context of the military conflict that will precede His coming.

ISRAEL'S GLORIOUS FUTURE

> Again I ask: Did they stumble so as to fall beyond recovery? Not at all! Rather, because of their transgression, salvation has come to the Gentiles to make Israel envious. But if their transgression means riches for the world, and their loss means riches for the Gentiles, how much greater riches will their full inclusion bring! (Rom. 11:11–12)

As previously explained, Paul pointed out how Gentiles are receiving a blessing because Israel rejected the gospel. Paul restated this in Romans 11:11–12.

The argument here is that if Israel being temporarily set aside has brought great riches to the Gentiles, how much more will the riches of God's grace be manifested when Israel will once again be restored. Just as Romans 9 deals with Israel's failures in the past and Romans 10 with their present opportunity to be saved, so Romans 11 paints a picture that Israel has a glorious future that will fulfill their expectation based on Old Testament prophecy.

ISRAEL'S RETURN TO BLESSING

> Consider therefore the kindness and sternness of God: sternness to those who fell, but kindness to you, provided that you continue in his kindness. Otherwise, you also will be cut off. And if they do not persist in unbelief, they will be grafted in, for God is able to graft them in again. After all, if you were cut out of an olive tree that is wild by nature, and contrary to nature were grafted into a culti-vated olive tree, how much more readily will these, the natural branches, be grafted into their own olive tree! (Rom. 11:22–24)

As Paul brought out, Gentiles have been grafted into the place of blessing, the olive tree. The Jews, on the other hand, have been temporarily cut off as a nation. However, it will be easier for Israel to be grafted into their own olive tree than it was for the Gentiles to be grafted in (Rom. 11:24).

The olive tree in Scripture represents the blessings that come through Abraham to both Jews and Gentiles. Because the Abrahamic covenant had provision for Gentile blessing (Gen. 12:3), it was possible for the Gentiles to be grafted in; but most of the promises that are involved in the Abrahamic covenant relate to the Jews, their future possession of the land, and their restoration spiritually. Accordingly, it is more natural for Israel to be grafted into the Abrahamic olive tree than it is for Gentiles.

ALL ISRAEL WILL BE SAVED

> I do not want you to be ignorant of this mystery, brothers and sisters, so that you may not be conceited: Israel has experienced a hardening in part until the full number of the Gentiles has come in, and in this way all Israel will be saved. As it is written:
>
> "The deliverer will come from Zion;
>   he will turn godlessness away from Jacob.
> And this is my covenant with them
>   when I take away their sins." (Rom. 11:25–27)

The outworking of God's present purpose of calling out both Jew and Gentile on an equal basis to form the body of Christ was not anticipated in the Old Testament. Its major features were mysteries, that is, truths that were not revealed in the Old Testament but were stated in the New Testament. Paul indicated he wanted Israel to understand this factor.

In God's program, the project of calling out His church of both Jews and Gentiles must be completed first (1 Cor. 12:12–13; Eph. 1:22–23; 4:11–13). What is being predicted in Romans 11:25–27 is that God will deliver Israel after His purpose for His church has been fulfilled. The reference to Israel being saved is not in respect to freedom from the guilt of sin or the redemptive truth but rather that Israel will be delivered from her enemies at the time of the second coming. As brought out in the quotation in verse 26 that a deliverer will come, this assures, on the one hand, a completion of God's purpose for the Gentiles and, on the other hand, Israel's restoration after this period is over. The answer to the question of whether God rejects His people (v. 1) is answered by the fact that God has not rejected them but will carry out His purposes as indicated in prophecy.

Prior to Israel's deliverance, however, during the present age they are experiencing a hardening of the heart, that is, many in Israel are turning away from the gospel. This will continue until God's purpose in His church is complete. Then there will be a revival in Israel and many will turn to the Lord.

The background of this is the New Testament doctrine of the rapture of the church. When the church is taken out of the world in fulfillment of God's purpose for the church, Israel's present experience of hardening will also be removed and revival will come to Israel (Rom. 11:25–26). Their early conversion to the gospel will help spread the gospel throughout the world after the rapture of the church as there are Israelites in every major nation who already know the languages and the people.

It is obvious from Scripture that not every individual Israelite will be saved from the guilt and power of sin. In Ezekiel 20:33–38, it is predicted that the rebels in Israel, those who were not saved prior to Christ's second coming, will be purged and only those converted will be allowed to enter the millennial kingdom. Accordingly, the deliverance in salvation referenced in Romans 11:26 refers to a national deliverance, that is, a cessation of their persecution by the Gentiles. Those delivered are not necessarily saved in the sense of being saved from the guilt and power of sin. Though some expositors labor to try to prove that Israel has no future, the whole of Romans 11 teaches otherwise. It predicts that Israel does have a future once God's present purpose is fulfilled in the church.

The quotation in Romans 11:26–27 is a combination of several verses in the Old Testament. What is being taught is that the Redeemer will come out of Zion, that He will turn ungodliness away from Jacob, and that this will be a fulfillment of God's promise to extend mercy and salvation to Israel.

The Old Testament speaks of Christ's coming to Zion as well as coming from Zion (Pss. 14:7; 20:2; 53:6; 110:2; 128:5; 134:3, 135:21; Isa. 2:3; Joel 3:16; Amos 1:2). The point is that in the second coming, Christ will come to Zion both to rule over Israel and to rule the world, including the Gentiles. Zion here is used as a reference to Jerusalem, as is common in Scripture.

The fulfillment predicted in Romans 11:25–27 is in keeping with the Abrahamic covenant, which promises that Israel will endure as a nation forever and that ultimately the Israelites will be restored spiritually and to their land politically. Though this truth is opposed by some scholars who do not accept the concept of a millennial kingdom after the second coming, the only way to understand these passages, dealing with truths such as the Scripture presents here, is to take literally the facts that Israel has a future as a nation and that her future is linked to the second coming of Christ.

In the verses that follow (Rom. 11:28–32), a further statement is given of God's plan to give mercy to Israel and the certainty of that being fulfilled in the future. Chapter 11 of Romans closes with a remarkable statement of the wisdom of God in dealing with His purposes in the world, and especially in regard to Israel.

THE WOMAN WITH CHILD

> A great sign appeared in heaven: a woman clothed
> with the sun, with the moon under her feet and a
> crown of twelve stars on her head. She was pregnant
> and cried out in pain as she was about to give birth.
> (Rev. 12:1–2)

The prophecy in Revelation 12 continues to be controversial and will therefore require a more lengthy explanation than the other prophecies in this chapter. One of the important problems in the interpretation of prophecy through the centuries of the church has been the tendency to take passages that relate to Israel and interpret them as dealing with the church in the present age. This problem appears in Revelation 12, as some have said the woman represents the church. In order to make this prophecy relate to the church, it requires nonliteral interpretation without any real fulfillment of the predictive elements. A far better explanation is that this relates to Israel, as this is supported by the details of the prophecy.

If the predictions of this portion of Revelation are to be interpreted properly, it is necessary to give close attention to the details concerning each person. In this case, the woman is not the church or Jesus Christ but is Israel seen as the matrix from which Jesus Christ came.

In Scripture, a woman is frequently used to represent different entities. For instance, Jezebel represents a false religion (Rev. 2:20). The prostitute of Revelation 17 is the apostate church of the end time. The bride, the Lamb's wife (19:7), represents the church joined to Christ in glory. Israel is also represented as the unfaithful wife of Jehovah. In this description, true Israel, or that portion of Israel standing true to God, is in view.

The statement that she is "clothed with the sun, with the moon under her feet" (Rev. 12:1) is an allusion to Joseph's dream in which he saw the sun, moon, and eleven stars bowing down to him (Gen. 37:9). The sun and the moon in this context refer to Jacob and Rachel, the forbearers of Israel. The woman is also said to have "a crown of twelve stars on her head" (Rev. 12:1). In Joseph's dream also the stars, or the sons of Israel, are intended with the twelfth star, including Joseph himself, who was not in the dream as such.

The fact that the woman is pregnant and in pain refers to the experience of Israel down through the centuries, awaiting the coming of her Messiah. Her sufferings refer to the nation as a whole, not to Mary the mother of Jesus.

In Revelation 12:4, a dragon is pictured as awaiting the birth of the child to devour it as soon as it is born. This, of course, refers to the birth of Christ and the attempts of Herod to destroy the infant Jesus. It was necessary for Joseph and Mary and Jesus to go to Egypt for the early years of Jesus's life in order to escape Herod's desire to destroy Him (Matt. 2:13–18).

John then recorded, "She gave birth to a son, a male child, who 'will rule all the nations with an iron scepter.' And her child was snatched up to God and to his throne. The woman fled into the wilderness to a place prepared for her by God, where she might be taken care of for 1,260 days" (Rev. 12:5–6).

The child is described as the one who "will rule all nations with an iron scepter" (v. 5). This is prophesied in Revelation 19:15 as referring to Christ and fulfilled in the millennial kingdom as predicted in Psalm 2:9: "You will break them with a rod of iron; you will dash them to pieces like pottery." Christ is also prophesied as the ruler over Israel but here is pictured in a more gentle fashion (Luke 1:32–33).

The statement that the child will be "snatched up to God and to his throne" (Rev. 12:5) has also been debated, some referring it to the deliverance from Egypt after Herod was dead. It is probable, however, that it refers to the ascension of Christ.

The statement "the woman fled into the wilderness to a place prepared for her by God, where she might be taken care of for 1,260 days" (v. 6) is a reference to Israel being preserved through the great tribulation. This is also predicted in Old Testament prophecy in Jeremiah 30:7: "How awful that day will be! No other will be like it. It will be a time of trouble for Jacob, but he will be saved out of it." The 1,260 days are the exact length of the great tribulation that will culminate in the second coming of Christ. Though many in

Israel will perish (Zech. 13:8), Israel as a nation will be preserved and be rescued by Christ when He comes (Ezek. 20:33–38; Rom. 11:26–27).

As we can see in this chapter, prophecies from both the Old Testament and the New Testament consistently predict when Israel will be restored in spite of its initial rejection of the Messiah. The opportunity for this will happen during Christ's millennial reign. Once Israel has been restored, it will be time for Christ's ultimate judgment, which we will explore in the next chapter.

7

JUDGMENT DAY

What will come of creation during the end times? What will happen to the earth, which we have been given to steward? What will happen in the heavens when these incredible events are set in motion? God, in His wisdom, has not left out any detail. Rather, Scripture is full of specific prophecies regarding Christ's judgment of all creation—things both ethereal and eternal.

THE CREATOR JUDGES THE CREATION

In Zephaniah 1:1–3, we read of the ultimate judgment of God on the entire earth at the time of the second coming of Christ. Zephaniah declared the word of the Lord: "'I will sweep away everything from the face of the earth,' declares the LORD. 'I will sweep away both man and beast; I will sweep away the birds of the sky and the fish in the sea—and the idols that cause the wicked to stumble. When I destroy all mankind on the face of the earth,' declares the LORD" (vv. 2–3).

GOD'S VERDICT ON JUDAH AND
JERUSALEM

Zephaniah declared the word of the Lord against Judah and
Jerusalem: "I will stretch out my hand against Judah and against all
who live in Jerusalem" (1:4). God particularly detailed that the "remnant of Baal" (v. 4) and the names of the idolatrous priests would be
judged: "I will destroy every remnant of Baal worship in this place,
the very names of the idolatrous priests—those who bow down on
the roofs to worship the starry host, those who bow down and swear
by the LORD and who also swear by Molek" (vv. 4–5).

Judah was compared to a prepared sacrifice (v. 7), and on the
day of the Lord, princes and those wearing foreign clothes would
especially be the objects of His wrath (vv. 7–8).

Zephaniah declared the word of the Lord: "Wail, you who live
in the market district; all your merchants will be wiped out, all who
trade with silver will be destroyed" (v. 11). Their houses would be
taken over by others, their vineyards would provide wine for others,
and their wealth would be plundered (vv. 12–13). The day of the
Lord was described in detail:

> The great day of the LORD is near—
>   near and coming quickly.
> The cry on the day of the LORD is bitter;
>   the Mighty Warrior shouts his battle cry.
> That day will be a day of wrath—
>   a day of distress and anguish,
> a day of trouble and ruin,

a day of darkness and gloom,
a day of clouds and blackness—
a day of trumpet and battle cry
against the fortified cities
and against the corner towers.

I will bring such distress on all people
that they will grope about like those who are
blind,
because they have sinned against the LORD.
(vv. 14–17)

These prophecies were fulfilled in history and will be fulfilled at the second coming.

JESUS HAS AUTHORITY TO SENTENCE AND PARDON

Because Jesus healed the invalid at the pool of Bethesda on the Sabbath, the Jews persecuted Him (John 5:2–16). Because Jesus claimed God as His Father, the Jews persecuted Him all the more because they regarded this as a statement that He was equal to the Father (vv. 17–18).

In His exposition on His union with the Father, Jesus declared that the Father loved Him (v. 20), that He had the power to raise the dead even as the Father did (v. 21), and that the Father had entrusted all judgment to the Son (vv. 22–23). Accordingly, whoever does not honor the Son does not honor the Father (v. 23).

This led Jesus to declare, "Very truly I tell you, whoever hears my word and believes him who sent me has eternal life and will not be judged but has crossed over from death to life" (v. 24).

Expanding further on His ability to save, Jesus said:

> Very truly I tell you, a time is coming and has now come when the dead will hear the voice of the Son of God and those who hear will live. For as the Father has life in himself, so he has granted the Son also to have life in himself. And he has given him authority to judge because he is the Son of Man.
>
> Do not be amazed at this, for a time is coming when all who are in their graves will hear his voice and come out—those who have done what is good will rise to live, and those who have done what is evil will rise to be condemned. (vv. 25–29)

The broad prophecies revealed by the Savior here predict, first of all, the salvation of individuals who hear the facts about Christ and as a result of believing will live eternally. Just as Jesus has life in Himself from the Father, so He has authority to judge as the Son of Man (v. 26). For further confirmation of Christ's ability, Jesus called attention to the fact that those in the grave, referring to those who have died physically, will someday hear His voice and come out of the grave with the result that they will be judged concerning their lives on earth, whether good or bad (vv. 28–29). In asserting this fact of judgment, Christ Jesus was not teaching that all the resurrections will occur at the same time, as other scriptures make clear that there will be a series of resurrections and the wicked will not be judged until all the righteous are raised.

In these predictions and assertions, the apostle John recorded one fact after another supporting his belief that Jesus was the Son of God and the only Savior who could give eternal life.

JUDGMENT: THE ULTIMATE CONSEQUENCE OF SIN

The doctrine of sin and guilt always has a present application while also implying future judgment. In dealing especially with Gentile sin and rebellion against God, Paul revealed a certain divine judgment in Romans 2:5–16. He stated:

> But because of your stubbornness and your unre-
> pentant heart, you are storing up wrath against
> yourself for the day of God's wrath, when his righ-
> teous judgment will be revealed. God "will repay
> each person according to what they have done." To
> those who by persistence in doing good seek glory,
> honor and immortality, he will give eternal life. But
> for those who are self-seeking and who reject the
> truth and follow evil, there will be wrath and anger.
> (vv. 5–8)

Earlier in Romans 2, Paul argued that everyone has fallen short of God's moral standards and therefore should not pass judgment on others. He summarized, "So when you, a mere human being, pass judgment on them and yet do the same things, do you think you will escape God's judgment?" (v. 3). Because all have sinned, as Paul made clear later in this epistle, salvation is by faith and by grace.

There is, however, a different quality of life in those who are saved from those who are not saved. Those who persist in being unrepentant, as Paul stated, face certain judgment from God. In speaking of "the day of God's wrath" (v. 5), Paul was not referring to any specific day though, as Scripture unfolds the series of judgments that will characterize the judgment of every person and the final judgment will come at the end of the millennial kingdom (Rev. 20:11–15). Those who are saved have a different quality of life that demonstrates they have come to God in repentance and faith. Accordingly, their manner of life will be rewarded and result in eternal life. The life of doing good and receiving eternal life is obviously not possible unless a person believes and accepts the truth of God's gospel (Rom. 2:6–8).

Though Paul was dealing primarily with Gentiles, he made it clear that Jews were in the same situation: "There will be trouble and distress for every human being who does evil: first for the Jew, then for the Gentile; but glory, honor and peace for everyone who does good: first for the Jew, then for the Gentile. For God does not show favoritism" (vv. 9–11). The difference between Jew and Gentile is that the Jew has been given the revelation of the law and the Gentile has not, but this does not change the fundamental requirements of doing what is right in God's sight.

Paul specifically addressed the distinction between those who sin who know the law and those who do not: "All who sin apart from the law will also perish apart from the law, and all who sin under the law will be judged by the law. For it is not those who hear the law who are righteous in God's sight, but it those who obey the law who will be declared righteous" (vv. 12–13).

Throughout his epistles, Paul used the word *law* in a number of different senses. The point he made was that those who were under the Mosaic law who were Jews would be judged by it and that the Gentiles had a general moral law, and if they were living in the will of God, they would, to some extent, conform to the Mosaic law in its moral teachings. Paul stated:

> (Indeed, when the Gentiles, who do not have the law, do by nature things required by the law, they are a law for themselves, even though they do not have the law. They show that the requirements of the law are written on their hearts, their consciences also bearing witness, and their thoughts sometimes accusing them and at other times even defending them.) This will take place on the day when God judges people's secrets through Jesus Christ, as my gospel declares. (Rom. 2:14–16)

Because everyone has a conscience that to some extent distinguishes right from wrong, and because God deals with people's hearts, even if they are not Jews under the Mosaic law, they will be judged on the moral code they recognize as witnessed by their consciences.

In dealing with the day of judgment, Paul had in mind that God would judge Christians at the time of the rapture, as brought out in his previous writing in 1 Corinthians 3:11–15; 9:24–27. The unsaved, however, will not be judged finally until after the millennial kingdom. In life, however, God also deals judgment to those who rebel against Him, and they experience the wrath of God as it is expressed in history. But the final judgment will determine the ultimate destiny of the soul. This will be evident especially at the great tribulation preceding the second coming of Christ.

STANDING BEFORE CHRIST'S JUDGMENT SEAT

In Romans 14, the subject is how "gray" areas in the Christian life should be handled. A case in point is the question as to whether the Christian in the time of Paul could eat meat that had been previously offered to idols. The Christian community was divided on this; some said meat was meat regardless what happened to it before they bought it, and others claimed that by buying it they participated in the worship of the idols it involved.

The exhortation that comes out of the situation is that we should not judge our Christian brethren, especially in areas where there is difference of opinion as to what is the right thing to do. As Paul pointed out, the important fact is that Christ died and was resurrected so that He might be Lord over both the dead and the living: "For this very reason, Christ died and returned to life so that he might be the Lord of both the dead and the living" (v. 9). In view of this, Paul declared that Christians should not judge one another, especially in the area of evaluating the ministry of a brother. "You, then, why do you judge your brother or sister? Or why do you treat them with contempt? For we will all stand before God's judgment seat" (v. 10).

Paul gave further exposition of the judgment seat of Christ in 1 Corinthians 3:11–15; 9:24–27; and 2 Corinthians 5:10. Inasmuch as all Christians will stand before the judgment seat of Christ to be evaluated, believers should concentrate on their own problems instead of on the problems of others.

The absolute certainty of this judgment is stated in a quotation from Isaiah 45:23: "'As surely as I live,' says the Lord, 'every knee will bow before me; every tongue will acknowledge God'" (Rom. 14:11). Scripture is clear in both the Old Testament and the New Testament that every individual will stand before God's judgment, not necessarily at the same time or for the same reason. The judgment at the judgment seat of Christ is for those who have been saved who will then be evaluated as to their contribution to the Lord's work.

Paul continued to summarize this in Romans 14: "So then, each of us will give an account of ourselves to God" (v. 12). The figure is that of a steward, or a trustee, who has responsibility for handling the business affairs of another and eventually reporting what the steward does with it. In life, Christians are endowed with spiritual and natural gifts that differ. No two Christians are exactly alike, and no two Christians have exactly the same opportunities, but each will be required to give an account for what he or she has done with them. Obviously, the more a person has, the greater the responsibility.

The issue here is not success or amount of success but rather the question of faithfulness in using properly what God has given an individual Christian. Inasmuch as this is the main problem in the Christian life, we should not turn aside to try to be judges of our fellow Christians, except as it may be required in certain circumstances. Instead, we should be preoccupied with the fact that our own lives are going to be judged, and we should give ourselves to things that will count in eternity.

WARNING AND REWARDS

Because the Thessalonian church was experiencing persecution from unbelievers, Paul assured them that, on the one hand, the righteous would be rewarded in the future and, on the other hand, the wicked would be punished (2 Thess. 1:5–10). Paul wrote, "All this is evidence that God's judgment is right, and as a result you will be counted worthy of the kingdom of God, for which you are suffering. God is just: He will pay back trouble to those who trouble you and give relief to you who are troubled, and to us as well" (vv. 5–7). The truth that God will judge everyone sometime in the future is taught in Scripture, but such a program is a comfort and a strength to those undergoing persecution because they know that they will be rewarded and blessed and that God will deal with their persecutors in judgment.

Our expectation appears in the further details of 2 Thessalonians in which we learn that God will "give relief to you who are troubled, and to us as well. This will happen when the Lord Jesus is revealed from heaven in blazing fire with his powerful angels. He will punish those who do not know God and do not obey the gospel of our Lord Jesus. They will be punished with everlasting destruction and shut out from the presence of the Lord and from the glory of his might" (vv. 7–9).

Scripture reveals that there are several times when God deals in direct judgment on the world. Some of these will occur in what is referred to as the great tribulation, the forty-two-month period before the second coming. Some will occur at the second coming of Christ when people, living in the world that rebels against God and does not put its trust in Christ, will be judged unworthy of the millennial kingdom and be purged. A further judgment is recorded in Revelation 20:11–15 in which the wicked dead will be raised and judged. This is the final judgment.

Some people question the notion that the wicked unbelievers persecuting the Thessalonian church will not receive their final punishment until the judgment of the great white throne (vv. 11–15). Those who are punished at the time of Christ's second coming will be those living at the time who are unbelievers, but will not include those who persecuted the Thessalonian church who, of course, have died. The exact time is not indicated here because there are several periods of divine judgment.

The Thessalonians were assured that, in God's time and in God's way, those who persecuted them would be punished, including their being shut out from the Lord. Because neither Paul nor the Thessalonian Christians knew when the Lord was coming, they could gather from this revelation the assurance that the wicked would be taken care of in God's program, whether sooner or later.

A further difficulty in explaining this passage is that this destruction is linked to the day of the Lord's glorification. According to 2 Thessalonians 1:10, the punishment of the wicked will be "on the day he comes to be glorified in his holy people and to be marveled at among all those who have believed. This includes you, because you believed our testimony to you."

The Lord will come at different times in the future program and will be glorified. He, first of all, was glorified when He went to heaven following His period on earth. He will be glorified and His majesty will be revealed also at the second coming when the world will be put under His power and judgment, and those who have trusted Him, referred to here as "his holy people," will be glorified. The glory of Christ again will be manifest at the end of the millennial kingdom at the great white throne judgment when He deals with the wicked dead and commits them to eternal punishment. Accordingly, the prophecy must be taken as not referring to a specific moment in the future program but to the fact that in the course of these various fulfillments of prophecy the wicked will be judged and Christ will be glorified.

THE CERTAINTY OF DIVINE JUDGMENT

A Christian living in this present age of grace is nevertheless reminded that it is part of God's righteous government that every individual will be judged. Normally, this is after his death: "Just as people are destined to die once, and after that to face judgment, so Christ was sacrificed once to take away the sins of many; and he will appear a second time, not to bear sin, but to bring salvation to those who are waiting for him" (Heb. 9:27–28). The coming judgment for all humans makes most clear the necessity of entering by faith into the grace of God, which is provided through the death of Christ. Though judgment is certain, those who have entered into grace at the present age will find that their judgment is a gracious judgment and will consist for believers as evaluations of their lives and service as a basis for reward, as brought out in the doctrine of the judgment seat of Christ (2 Cor. 5:10).

THE TREMBLING OF HEAVEN AND EARTH

In reviewing God's judgments in the past, a reminder is given that there is a future judgment coming: "At that time his voice shook the earth, but now he has promised, 'Once more I will shake not only the earth but also the heavens'" (Heb. 12:26). Prophetic scriptures expand on this in both the Old Testament and the New Testament and describe the terrible judgments that will shake the earth prior to the second coming of Christ. This will be part of God's program of judgment on the wicked and will also end in the blessing and rescue of those who are saved. A reminder of the fragile character of our present world is also a reminder that eternal things that belong to the Christian faith are not subject to change or destruction.

JUDGMENT OF FALSE TEACHERS

As Peter neared the end of his life, he was overwhelmed by the evidence of corruption in doctrine and departure from the faith on the part of those who were apostates, that is, people who outwardly claimed to be Christians but actually had no Christian faith. Accordingly, those who read 2 Peter, written shortly before his death, are warned that these teachers not only will reject the truth themselves but also will bring in teachings that are radical and destructive.

Peter described these false teachers:

> But there were also false prophets among the people,
> just as there will be false teachers among you. They
> will secretly introduce destructive heresies, even

denying the sovereign Lord who bought them—
bringing swift destruction on themselves. Many
will follow their depraved conduct and will bring
the way of truth into disrepute. In their greed these
teachers will exploit you with fabricated stories.
Their condemnation has long been hanging over
them, and their destruction has not been sleeping.
(2 Pet. 2:1–3)

In dealing with heresies, Peter was not describing minor devia-
tions from the faith but that which was essential to salvation and
hope. The false teachers will be guilty of "even denying the sovereign
Lord who bought them" (v. 1).

Of significance in this passage is the word for *redemption*, translated "bought," that is used even for these false teachers. Scholars
debate whether it includes everyone. This is one of the central passages that demonstrates when Christ died He died to make the whole
world savable, dying even for those who do not turn to Christ and
accept His proffered salvation. The condemnation of the wicked is all
the greater because Christ died for them and they rejected that which
He provided for them in grace.

The condemnation of the false teachers was seen in the light
of God's judgment on the angels, for whom there was no grace or
mercy:

For if God did not spare angels when they sinned,
but sent them to hell, putting them in chains of
darkness to be held for judgment; if he did not

spare the ancient world when he brought the
flood on its ungodly people, but protected Noah,
a preacher of righteousness, and seven others; if he
condemned the cities of Sodom and Gomorrah by
burning them to ashes, and made them an example
of what is going to happen to the ungodly; and if
he rescued Lot, a righteous man, who was distressed
by the depraved conduct of the lawless (for that
righteous man, living among them day after day,
was tormented in his righteous soul by the lawless
deeds he saw and heard)—if this is so, then the
Lord knows how to rescue the godly from trials and
to hold the unrighteous for punishment on the day
of judgment. (2 Pet. 2:4–9)

Accordingly, if Christians are tormented by the terrible sins of
the unsaved world, as Lot was in his day, they can rest assured, with
Lot, that God's judgment in His proper time will take care of the
wicked.

The utter lack of moral character of the wicked was described
further in that they "heap abuse on celestial beings" (v. 10) in their
slanderous accusations against such beings in the presence of the
Lord (v. 11) and in their blasphemy in essential doctrine "they do
not understand" (v. 12), though "they are blots and blemishes, revel-
ing in their pleasures while they feast with you" (v. 13). Although
it is true that their "eyes" are "full of adultery" and "they seduce the
unstable" (v. 14), they will be judged in God's time and brought into
proper punishment for their deeds.

Comparison is made between these false teachers and Balaam, a prophet of God (Num. 22) who was hired to curse Israel though he was kept from it (2 Pet. 2:15–16). These false teachers "are springs without water and mists driven by a storm. Blackest darkness is reserved for them" (v. 17). Their winning oratory and their promise of freedom are not supported, and those who follow them will become "worse off at the end than they were at the beginning" (v. 20). This scathing denial of apostate teachers reflects God's approach to this important aspect of modern life in which many reject the Word of God and substitute man-made religions instead. Peter assured believers that though in this life we may suffer persecution and trial, in the end the righteous will triumph and the wicked will perish.

THE GREAT WHITE THRONE JUDGMENT

John then recorded the change in the scene and introduced the revelation concerning the great white throne and the judgment of the wicked dead (Rev. 20:11–15). He wrote, "Then I saw a great white throne and him who was seated on it. The earth and the heavens fled from his presence, and there was no place for them" (v. 11). Though the word *throne* appears some thirty times in the book of Revelation, the instance here is a reference to a throne different from any previously mentioned, and accordingly, it is called "a great white throne." Unlike the previous thrones on earth or heaven, it is pictured as being in space and occupied by Christ Himself.

This is supported by the statement in John 5:22–23: "Moreover, the Father judges no one, but has entrusted all judgment to the Son, that all may honor the Son just as they honor the Father. Whoever does not honor the Son does not honor the Father, who sent him." Like the judgment seat of Christ that took place in heaven before the millennium, this judgment does not have its scene on earth but in space.

The fact that earth and sky ("heavens") fled from the presence of the One on the throne is in keeping with Revelation 21:1 in which a new heaven and a new earth are introduced. As John watched, he saw this great judgment taking place:

> And I saw the dead, great and small, standing before the throne, and books were opened. Another book was opened, which is the book of life. The dead were judged according to what they had done as recorded in the books. The sea gave up the dead that were in it, and death and Hades gave up the dead that were in them, and each person was judged according to what they had done. Then death and Hades were thrown into the lake of fire. The lake of fire is the second death. Anyone whose name was not found written in the book of life was thrown into the lake of fire. (Rev. 20:12–15)

As this text makes plain, this is the final judgment. As the righteous have already been judged, this judgment relates to the wicked. This is the final resurrection in contrast to the first resurrection, which has to do with the righteous (Dan. 12:2; John 5:29; Acts 24:15; Rev. 20:5).

The fact that both small and great are specified is similar to descriptions previously used in Revelation (11:18; 13:16; 19:5, 18).

Those standing before the throne come from all walks of life but now are being judged on the basis of their works. According to Hebrews 9:27, everyone has to face Christ in judgment. The judgment is based on what occurs in the books that record their works and whether their names are in the Book of Life.

The Book of Life is presented as including the names of all who are genuinely saved. The description of this resurrection indicates that it is a universal resurrection of all who are yet in the grave, that is, the unrighteous. Special mention is made of the sea as giving up the dead in it because bodies lost at sea disintegrate and are scattered as far as the particles of their human bodies are concerned. This is no problem for an omnipotent God, and their bodies are raised from the dead in the sea. Hades is also declared to give up the dead that are in it (Rev. 20:13), and those in Hades are thrown into the lake of fire.

Distinction in Scripture should be observed between Hades, which is the place of the dead in between death and resurrection, and the lake of fire, which is the final destiny of those who are unsaved. The resurrection of the wicked is distinguished from the resurrection of the righteous in that there is no reward or recognition of righteousness on their part.

Like the righteous, they are given bodies that cannot be destroyed. But while the righteous receive bodies that are holy and suited for the presence of God, the wicked dead receive bodies that are indestructible and suited for eternal punishment. They are still wicked and still in rebellion against God. Scripture is very clear that those whose names are not found in the Book of Life will be thrown into the lake of fire.

Many have attempted to find some escape for the wicked so that they would not be the objects of eternal punishment. From a human viewpoint, this may be desired, but the Bible never suggests that the punishment of the wicked continues only for a time. If the beast and the false prophet after one thousand years in the lake of fire are still intact, it is obvious that those who are now being thrown into the lake of fire will, likewise, continue in the place of torment. Christ Himself emphasized the destiny of the wicked (Matt. 13:42; 25:41, 46). In Revelation 14:11, those who received the mark of the beast were declared to be the objects of eternal punishment. Scriptural revelation limits the destiny of mankind to either heaven or the lake of fire.

8

REWARDS OF THE RIGHTEOUS

It's no wonder that for many believers the portrait painted in Scripture of the end times can bring a sense of unease. Although we put our trust in the Lord and have confidence in His mercy, we know that the end times will bring trials and tribulation. Thankfully, the Lord has given us many reassurances that we can cling to when we are tempted to fear. The following passages paint a portrait we can fix our eyes on when we need to be reminded of our future hope.

THE PROMISE OF ETERNAL LIFE

When Jesus testified to Nicodemus concerning the difficulty of accepting spiritual truth, He stated, "Just as Moses lifted up the snake in the wilderness, so the Son of Man must be lifted up, that everyone who believes may have eternal life in him. For God so loved the world that he gave his one and only Son, that whoever believes in him shall not perish but have eternal life" (John 3:14–16). In alluding to Moses's lifting up the snake in the wilderness, Jesus was referring to Numbers 21:6–9. When the children of Israel complained about not having food and water to their liking, Numbers recorded that

God sent venomous snakes among the people and caused many to die (v. 6). When the people of Israel confessed that they had sinned, the Lord instructed Moses to make a bronze snake and place it on a pole, and if the people were bitten by the snakes, they could look at the bronze snake and be healed (vv. 8–9).

Using this historical illustration, Jesus declared that He also "must be lifted up" (John 3:14). Just as in the case of Israel when they looked at the bronze serpent in faith and were healed, so Jesus predicted that when they looked at Him lifted up, they would believe and have eternal life (v. 15). In speaking of being lifted up, Jesus was referring to His crucifixion and the need for them to go to the cross in faith in order to have salvation through Him. Jesus concluded this with the great affirmation that the gift of God's Son was an act of love and that "whoever believes in him shall not perish but have eternal life" (v. 16). No doubt, the disciples did not understand what Jesus was referring to until after His death and resurrection.

As a summary of this important chapter, the apostle John declared, "Whoever believes in the Son has eternal life, but whoever rejects the Son will not see life, for God's wrath remains on them" (v. 36). This verse provides a marvelous prophecy that belief in Jesus as the Son assures an individual of eternal life in contrast to those who reject Jesus, who not only do not receive life but also are under God's wrath.

A RIGHTEOUS REWARD

Christians are exhorted to serve the Lord even as slaves serve their masters. If anything, a Christian should do better (Eph. 6:7–9).

As Paul expressed it, "Serve wholeheartedly, as if you were serving the Lord, not people" (v. 7). In their service for God, Christians are assured that the Lord will reward them for what has been done, and this is regardless of whether one is a slave or free (v. 8). In view of the ultimate reward of the church in heaven, earthly masters are urged to treat their earthly slaves in a kind way (v. 9).

OUR NEW, GLORIFIED BODIES

In contrast to the wicked, whose destiny is destruction, though not annihilation, Paul referred to the fact that Christians are citizens of heaven.

Their expectation is in the future with the ultimate goal that they will have a glorious body in heaven. "But our citizenship is in heaven. And we eagerly await a Savior from there, the Lord Jesus Christ, who, by the power that enables him to bring everything under his control, will transform our lowly bodies so that they will be like his glorious body" (Phil. 3:20–21). Though Christians are still on earth, they are citizens of heaven and are governed by the unseen power of God working in their lives.

The same power that enables Christians to bring their lives under control will also ultimately transform their bodies in this life to bodies "like his glorious body" (v. 21).

Paul was referring here to the fact that a believer's resurrection body will be patterned after the resurrection body of Christ. This body will be a body of flesh and bone but a body without sin, decay, or death. In speaking of the believer's body as a glorious body, it does not mean that our bodies will emanate brilliant light, as is sometimes true of God Himself, as in the transfiguration of Christ, and as revealed of God in heaven. The glory of which Philippians 3 is speaking about here is in reference to the fact that the glory of God is the manifestation of His infinite perfections. Though believers may not have bodies that glow with light in a similar way as the transfigured body of Christ did (Matt. 17:1–2), their bodies will nevertheless reflect God's perfections.

A Christian's resurrection body will therefore be holy as God is holy, immortal as God is immortal, everlasting as God is everlasting, and a constant reminder of the extent of God's grace that took those who were justifiably destined for eternal punishment and transformed them into saints whose resurrection or translation introduced them to a life wholly committed to God.

AN INHERITANCE FROM THE LORD

After exhorting all classes of Christians—husbands, wives, children, fathers, and slaves—to living a life in keeping with their faith in Christ, the apostle added the promise, "Whatever you do, work at it with all your heart, as working for the Lord, not for human masters, since you know that you will receive an inheritance from the Lord as a reward. It is the Lord Christ you are serving" (Col. 3:23–24).

Though all Christians will have an inheritance in Christ because it is based fundamentally on grace, it is nevertheless true that our inheritance is also a reward for faithful service to God in this present world. The point is that God is not settling all accounts now, and in heaven there will be reward for those who did not receive their reward in life.

THE PROMISE OF THE CROWN OF LIFE

Those who will trust in the Lord in a time of trial are especially blessed: "Blessed is the one who perseveres under trial because, having stood the test, that person will receive the crown of life that the Lord has promised to those who love him" (James 1:12). Believers will be rewarded in heaven for their faithfulness to the Lord. Often these rewards are characterized as crowns (1 Cor. 9:25; Phil. 4:1; 1 Thess. 2:19; 2 Tim. 4:8; 1 Pet. 5:4; Rev. 2:10; 3:11; 4:4, 10). The persecutions may bring humiliation and suffering on earth, but the fact that we have eternal life will be a crown that will set us apart as belonging to the Lord.

THE CERTAINTY OF OUR INHERITANCE

In keeping with the "living hope" given Christians "through the resurrection of Jesus Christ," they have a future inheritance "that can never perish, spoil or fade. [And] this inheritance is kept in heaven for you" (1 Pet. 1:3–4). Meanwhile, as Christians are waiting for their inheritance, God protects them: "who through faith are shielded by God's power until the coming of the salvation that is ready to be revealed in the last time" (v. 5). This inheritance is certain because of God's promise in grace. Peter went on to say that persecutions and trials in Christ demonstrate the genuineness of a believer's faith.

A PROMISED WELCOME INTO GOD'S KINGDOM

In making sure that our faith in Christ is real, Christians are reminded we "will receive a rich welcome into the eternal kingdom of our Lord and Savior Jesus Christ" (2 Pet. 1:11). Though the world may not always welcome Christians and our testimony, and there may be opposition and even a martyr's death, as in the case of Peter, it is still true that we can anticipate, either through death or through rapture, that we will be received and publicly acknowledged as a part of God's kingdom.

BELIEVERS WILL SHARE CHRIST'S THRONE

At the conclusion of the seven messages to the churches, a general invitation was given to those who would listen and come to Christ (Rev. 3:19–21). First of all, Christ stated the general principle: "Those whom I love I rebuke and discipline. So be earnest and repent" (v. 19). As is illustrated in the messages to the churches, Christ said that His purpose was not to judge but to bring them to repentance. An interesting fact is that He addressed them as "those whom I love." The important fact is His rebuke and discipline stem from His love for them. The word *discipline* has in it the thought of child training taken from childhood to adulthood. The exhortation to self-judgment and repentance is another reminder that Christians who do not judge themselves will be judged, as stated by Paul in 1 Corinthians 11:31–32: "For if we would judge ourselves, we would not be judged. But when we are judged, we are chastened by the Lord, that we may not be condemned with the world" (NKJV). Because the believer has established an eternal relationship with God as one who is saved, it is revealed that God will not allow the believer to continue in sin indefinitely, but sooner or later, either in time or eternity, will deal with the person.

Having urged them to have fellowship with Him, Christ then described Himself as One who is waiting for them to come: "Here I am! I stand at the door and knock. If anyone hears my voice and opens the door, I will come in and eat with that person, and they with me" (Rev. 3:20). This passage has sometimes been construed to refer to salvation, but in the context it seems to refer to those who already are believers. The issue is not related to salvation by eating with Christ but to fellowship, nourishment, and spiritual growth. God does not force Himself on anyone but waits for believers to come in simple faith to receive from God that which only God can supply.

The concept of knocking and entering is found in Scripture, of which Luke 12:35–40 is an illustration. However, in this and many other instances, the thought is that Christ is on the outside and the others who are on the inside waiting for Him to arrive should open the door when He comes. Christ used this in a parable: "Be dressed ready for service and keep your lamps burning, like servants waiting for their master to return from a wedding banquet, so that when he comes and knocks they can immediately open the door for him" (vv. 35–36).

The invitation Christ extends here for those who wish to come and eat with Him is a most gracious invitation and illustrates that fellowship with God is always available to those who are willing to put their trust in Christ and come to God. In that fellowship they will enjoy not only the presence of the Savior but also the nourishment and the strengthening that come from partaking of spiritual truth. They can be strengthened by dining on the things of God, the things of salvation, our wonderful hope, God's sustaining grace, and all the other blessings that are ours in Christ.

As Christ expressed it, "To the one who is victorious, I will give the right to sit with me on my throne, just as I was victorious and sat down with my Father on his throne" (Rev. 3:21). Those who walk with Christ in fellowship in this life will also enjoy the right of fellowship and sharing in the throne of Christ in eternity to come. This invitation is extended to any in the churches who are faithful and who honor and serve the Lord. It is another illustration of the gracious provision God has made for those who trust Him.

The message to the churches closes with the same invitation repeated in the message for each church: "Whoever has ears, let them hear what the Spirit says to the churches" (v. 22). God has spoken in words that should not be misunderstood, but so much depends on individuals hearing and responding to what they hear. The tragedy is that in so many cases no one is listening.

Taken as a whole, the messages to the seven churches represent the major spiritual problems of the church down through the ages. Ephesus represented the danger of forsaking the love that character-ized believers when they first trusted Christ (2:4). Smyrna illustrated the danger of fear, though otherwise they were faithful to God (v. 10). The church at Pergamum served as a reminder of the constant dan-ger of doctrinal compromise (vv. 14–15). The church at Thyatira illustrated moral compromise (v. 20). The church at Sardis showed the danger of spiritual deadness (3:1–2). The church at Philadelphia, though faithful, was warned to hold fast to the things that they believed (v. 11). And Laodicea illustrated the danger of being luke-warm (vv. 15–16), of outer religion without inner zeal and reality.

Though the book of Revelation deals primarily with prophecy concerning the future, it was written to help the churches of the present age understand the purposes of God and the great events that will characterize the end of the age.

9

THE FALL OF SATAN

From the start of human history, Satan has been a persistent adversary of God's people. His name originally meant "accuser," and indeed, every Christian can testify to living beneath the weight of Satan's constant accusations. But thankfully, his accusations are rendered void in light of the redemption of the cross.

Satan's role in human history has been important, and so his ultimate demise at the end time will be just as significant.

ORIGINAL JUDGMENT ON SATAN

> So the LORD God said to the serpent, "Because you
> have done this,
>
> "Cursed are you above all livestock
>   and all wild animals!
> You will crawl on your belly
>   and you will eat dust
>   all the days of your life.

And I will put enmity
>> between you and the woman,
>> and between your offspring and hers;
> he will crush your head,
>> and you will strike his heel."
>> (Gen. 3:14–15)

From the dawn of human history, Satan has been against us, and his adversarial role started in Genesis.

In fulfilling the prophecy of death, God added other prophecies, including the curse on the serpent (Gen. 3:14–15). God prophesied that Eve would give birth to children in pain and that her husband would rule over her. To Adam, God predicted that the ground would be cursed and he would have difficulty raising the food necessary for his continued existence.

Among these promises, which increased the judgment that had come on mankind because of the entrance of sin, a plan for redemption was also revealed.

In pronouncing the curse on the Devil and the serpent, it was prophesied that there would always be enmity between the serpent and the descendants of the woman (v. 15). Referring to one of the woman's descendants (Christ), God said, "He will crush your head." In regard to the judgment on Satan, made sure by the cross of Christ, the prophecy was further detailed, "You will strike his heel" (v. 15). This referred to the fact that Christ would die, but unlike the effect on Satan, His death would be conquered by resurrection. This was fulfilled in Christ's death and resurrection (Rom. 3:24–25).

THE TIMELESS STRUGGLE BETWEEN SATAN AND GOD

> How you have fallen from heaven,
>> morning star, son of the dawn!
> You have been cast down to the earth,
>> you who once laid low the nations!
> You said in your heart,
>> "I will ascend to the heavens;
> I will raise my throne
>> above the stars of God;
> I will sit enthroned on the mount of assembly,
>> on the utmost heights of Mount Zaphon.
> I will ascend above the tops of the clouds;
>> I will make myself like the Most High."
> But you are brought down to the realm of the
>> dead,
>> to the depths of the pit. (Isa. 14:12–15)

Some interpreters consider Isaiah 14:3–15 as referring to more than King Sennacherib and actually as a description of the fall of Satan in the prehistoric world. Satan, originally created as a holy angel, rebelled against God and was condemned to the perpetual judgment of God. The wording of verses 13–14 would describe very accurately the viewpoint of Satan in his desire to be raised above all other rulers and made "like the Most High" (v. 14). This form of revelation is often found in prophecy. In addition to the historical reference, this passage speaks of the larger struggle between Satan and God.

THE ACTIVITY OF SATAN

> I will not say much more to you, for the prince
> of this world is coming. He has no hold over me,
> but he comes so that the world may learn that I
> love the Father and do exactly what my Father has
> commanded me. (John 14:30–31)

By "prince of this world," Jesus was referring to Satan, and in this passage He pointed out the continued activity of Satan during the period when Jesus was going back to the Father. The ultimate triumph over Satan, however, was assured.

SATAN WILL BE CRUSHED

> The God of peace will soon crush Satan under your
> feet. (Rom. 16:20)

In connection with the greetings to various Christians in Rome, in which Paul exhorted them to serve the Lord with their full hearts, he prophesied, "The God of peace will soon crush Satan under your feet" (Rom. 16:20). Because the present age is of indeterminate length, and its length was unknown to Paul and others in the first century, it appeared to them that the final conquering of Satan would occur at the second coming of Christ and would be confirmed at the end of the millennium. Throughout the history of the church, these prophecies have had the quality of being soon, or imminent, as the duration of the present age is of unknown length.

Taken as a whole, the epistle to the Romans not only sets forth the great doctrines of sin, salvation, and sanctification but also explains how these doctrines affect Israel in the present age and in the future, when Israel's restoration is assured.

PROTECTION FROM THE EVIL ONE

In view of the problems of being easily deceived by false teachers as well as other problems in the Christian life, Paul requested prayer that he and his companions "may be delivered from wicked and evil people, for not everyone has faith" (2 Thess. 3:2). As Paul anticipated God's faithfulness in meeting his needs in answer to prayer, he also had confidence that the Thessalonian church would be strengthened and protected from the evil one (v. 3). His prayer for the Thessalonians was that they would continue in God's love and continue to serve the Lord (vv. 4–5).

SATAN, THE DRAGON WHO FIGHTS JESUS AT THE SECOND COMING

> Then war broke out in heaven. Michael and his angels fought against the dragon, and the dragon and his angels fought back. But he was not strong enough, and they lost their place in heaven. The great dragon was hurled down—that ancient serpent called the devil, or Satan, who leads the whole world astray. He was hurled to the earth, and his angels with him. (Rev. 12:7–9)

The beginning of the great tribulation, which is Israel's special time of trouble, is also marked by war in heaven. Earlier, the Roman Empire is pictured as the dragon (Rev. 12:4), but here the dragon is identified as Satan himself, who especially is in control of the world government at the period before the second coming. Until this event takes place, Satan is allowed in heaven and accuses the brethren as he did in the case of Job. The casting of Satan to the earth also marks the beginning of the most awful period in human history, the great tribulation.

John recorded the voice from heaven commemorating this event:

> Now have come the salvation and the power
>> and the kingdom of our God,
>> and the authority of his Messiah.
> For the accuser of our brothers and sisters,
>> who accuses them before our God day and
>>> night,
>> has been hurled down.
> They triumphed over him
>> by the blood of the Lamb
>> and by the word of their testimony;
> they did not love their lives so much
>> as to shrink from death.
> Therefore rejoice, you heavens
>> and you who dwell in them!
> But woe to the earth and the sea,
>> because the devil has gone down to you!

He is filled with fury,

because he knows that his time is short.

(vv. 10–12)

The long activity of Satan in heaven now comes to its close and with it the intensified activities of Satan on earth. Those who overcame Satan did so "by the blood of the Lamb," their faithful testimony, and their willingness to be martyrs if necessary (v. 11). On earth there would continue to be many martyrs through the great tribulation. Additionally, Satan knows prophecy and believes "his time is short" (v. 12).

Further attention is given to the activities of Satan during the great tribulation. John recorded, "When the dragon saw that he had been hurled to the earth, he pursued the woman who had given birth to the male child. The woman was given the two wings of a great eagle, so that she might fly to the place prepared for her in the wilderness, where she would be taken care of for a time, times and half a time, out of the serpent's reach" (vv. 13–14).

The time period here is the same as the 1,260 days mentioned earlier as the term *time* refers to one year, *times*, two years, plus a half time or a total of three and a half years (see also Dan. 7:25; 12:7). As previously explained, though many in Israel will perish as warned by Christ (Matt. 24:15–22), some believe there will be a specific place in the desert ("wilderness," Rev. 12:14) where Israel can flee; others take it as representative of the safety of those who survive. The description of Satan as the Devil has in it the thought of slandering or defaming and is used some fourteen times in the book of Job as well as elsewhere in Scripture (1 Chron. 21:1; Ps. 109:6;

Zech. 3:1–2). Satan is the opponent of Christ, and just as Christ defends the believers, Satan accuses them.

Though the power of Satan is tremendous, so is the strength given believers in that hour who are said to conquer through the blood of the Lamb and their testimony.

The flood in Revelation 12:15 that issues from Satan is probably symbolic of all that Satan is doing to destroy Israel. This would include false teaching that in the end time will come in like a flood. Circumstances of the great tribulation also would test their faith sorely in the fulfillment of the promise of the Messiah's coming. Satan attempts to persecute not only Israel but all others who obey God's commandments. This is, of course, illustrated in Revelation 7:9–17 and the many scriptures that speak of the horrors of the great tribulation.

From the standpoint of time, Revelation 12 has to be considered as occurring before chapter 6 if this is the time of the great tribulation. Parenthetic sections that deal with specific subjects are not chronological in their presentation but give a broad view of the activities of the period.

SATAN RELEASED FROM PRISON

When the thousand years are over, Satan will be released from his prison and will go out to deceive the nations in the four corners of the earth—Gog and Magog—and to gather them for battle. In number they are like the sand on the seashore. They marched across the breadth of the earth and

surrounded the camp of God's people, the city
he loves. But fire came down from heaven and
devoured them. (Rev. 20:7–9)

At the end of the millennium, Satan will be released and will go
out and deceive the nations (Rev. 20:7–8). The nations are referred
to as "Gog and Magog" (v. 8). This has confused some who try to
connect this with Ezekiel 38–39. But the war of Ezekiel is an invasion of Israel from the north by Russia and a few other nations. By a
series of judgments from God, the armies are completely wiped out
and months are spent in burying the bodies.

The battle in Revelation 20 is totally different. Those who form
the attackers come from all nations of the world, not just a few. They
gather about Jerusalem in an attempt to capture the capital city, but
fire comes down from heaven and devours them. The war of Ezekiel
38–39 is far north of Jerusalem.

The time situation is also different. The war of Ezekiel 38–39
occurs at a time when Israel is at peace and not expecting war. The
battle in Revelation 20 is at the end of the millennial kingdom and is
Satan's final attempt to conquer the world. There is no need to bury
the dead bodies because they have been consumed by fire in contrast to
Ezekiel 38–39. Life does not go on after this battle as in Ezekiel, for the
world moves immediately into the new heaven and new earth situation.

As we covered at the end of chapter 5, people have asked the question why Satan would be loosed from his prison after one thousand
years. This action is in keeping with God's purpose to demonstrate
in history that people left to their own devices will, nevertheless,
sin against God. Even though the millennium provided a perfect

environment for humanity with abundant revelation of God's power, the evil heart of man is manifest in the fact that people reject this and follow Satan when he is loose. The releasing of Satan also is a demonstration of the wickedness of Satan and the fallen angels and how even one thousand years in confinement does not change this.

SATAN CAST INTO A LAKE OF FIRE

> And the devil, who deceived them, was thrown into
> the lake of burning sulfur, where the beast and the
> false prophet had been thrown. They will be tor-
> mented day and night for ever and ever. (Rev. 20:10)

The wickedness of Satan is the basis for justifying God's judgment on Satan, who will be "thrown into the lake of burning sulfur" (Rev. 20:10). Important to note is the fact that the beast and the false prophet, who had been thrown into the lake of burning sulfur one thousand years before, are still there, demonstrating that this is not annihilation, but continued punishment. The beast and the false prophet as well as the Devil are included in the statement, "They will be tormented day and night for ever and ever" (v. 10).

Satan has been the fierce enemy of God and His people since the beginning of time, and he has caused untold misery and mayhem. To all the believers who have endured suffering because of Satan and his fallen followers, we can take courage that in the end he will get exactly what's coming to him. God will mete out justice, and the evil one will be banished for eternity.

10

HEAVEN, OUR ETERNAL HOME

At the end of all of these horrific events is the "thing you've all been waiting for"—life eternal with our Creator. While the Bible gives us few specific details about heaven, Scripture does paint a picture of a place where we will be restored to God's original vision for His relationship with us.

THE PROMISE OF AN ETERNAL HOUSE IN HEAVEN

In his second letter to the Corinthians, Paul unfolded the great truth that our present earthly bodies, which are so temporary, will be replaced by bodies that will last forever (5:1). Our present bodies have limitations and are subject to pain, illness, and death, and Christians long to have their permanent bodies: "Meanwhile we groan, longing to be clothed instead with our heavenly dwelling, because when we are clothed, we will not be found naked" (vv. 2–3). As Paul stated it, the "mortal may be swallowed up by life" (v. 4).

In facing the question as to whether Christians can be absolutely certain of their future resurrection, Paul pointed out that God has given us His Holy Spirit, the indwelling of which is our seal and assurance of future resurrection (Eph. 4:30). As Paul stated here, "Now the one who has fashioned us for this very purpose is God, who has given us the Spirit as a deposit, guaranteeing what is to come" (2 Cor. 5:5).

For Christians, there are two different states. While in their present bodies, Christians are physically away from the Lord in that they are not in His presence in heaven: "Therefore we are always confident and know that as long as we are at home in the body we are away from the Lord. For we live by faith, not by sight" (vv. 6–7).

The alternative of being with the Lord is attractive. However, as Paul had written earlier to the Philippians, "If I am to go on living in the body, this will mean fruitful labor for me. Yet what shall I choose? I do not know! I am torn between the two: I desire to depart and be with Christ, which is better by far; but it is more necessary for you that I remain in the body. Convinced of this, I know that I will remain, and I will continue with all of you for your progress and joy in the faith, so that through my being with you again your boasting in Christ Jesus will abound on account of me" (Phil. 1:22–26).

Paul stated, however, that while he was still in the body and in this life, "we make it our goal to please him, whether we are at home in the body or away from it" (2 Cor. 5:9). Our present life presents opportunities for service and reward that will not be open to us in the intermediate state between death and resurrection or after resurrection in heaven.

THE THRONE IN HEAVEN

> And there before me was a throne in heaven with someone sitting on it. And the one who sat there had the appearance of jasper and ruby. A rainbow that shone like an emerald encircled the throne. Surrounding the throne were twenty-four other thrones, and seated on them were twenty-four elders. They were dressed in white and had crowns of gold on their heads. From the throne came flashes of lightning, rumblings and peals of thunder. In front of the throne, seven lamps were blazing. These are the seven spirits of God. Also in front of the throne there was what looked like a sea of glass, clear as crystal. (Rev. 4:2–6)

John's first experience upon arrival in heaven was to behold "a throne in heaven with someone sitting on it" (Rev. 4:2). He described the personage on the throne in these words: "And the one who sat there had the appearance of jasper and ruby. A rainbow that shone like an emerald encircled the throne" (v. 3). The personage on the throne is said to resemble in His glory a jasper stone and a ruby. The jasper described in 21:11 is a clear stone in contrast to the opaque jasper stone known on earth. Accordingly, some have concluded that it may be a diamond in appearance.

Though the colors of the stones, enhanced by a rainbow that resembled an emerald, provide the glorious appearance, the significance of these stones may be derived from their use in Israel. On the breastplate of the priest were twelve stones, each representing a tribe of Israel. The ruby (or carnelian stone) and jasper were the first and last of the twelve stones, respectively (Exod. 28:17–21). Further, the jasper represented the tribe of Reuben, the first tribe, and the ruby represented Benjamin, the youngest tribe. Mention of these two stones, accordingly, was intended to include all the twelve tribes of Israel.

Moreover, the names of Reuben and Benjamin have significance because Reuben has the meaning of "behold the son" and Benjamin means "son of my right hand." Christ, of course, fulfills both of these functions, and He is the first begotten Son. Like Benjamin, He is "the Son of My right hand," also speaking of Christ in His relationship to God the Father. Taking all these things into consideration, it would seem best to interpret this passage as a description of God the Father sitting on a throne. This is also supported by the fact that Christ is pictured in a different way in this passage as separate from the One on the throne, though actually He occupies the throne with the Father also. The main purpose of this vision, however, is to show the glory of God.

As John surveyed the scene in heaven, he also saw twenty-four other thrones and recorded, "Surrounding the throne were twenty-four other thrones, and seated on them were twenty-four elders. They were dressed in white and had crowns of gold on their heads" (Rev. 4:4). They are obviously a representative group. In Israel, for instance, the many priests were divided into twenty-four groups, and one priest would represent each of the twenty-four. These twenty-four elders represent all the saints, both Old Testament and New Testament, or only the church of the present age, or perhaps they are angelic figures. Scholars have advanced these and other interpretations.

They were described as having white robes, speaking of righteousness in the presence of God, and wearing crowns of gold, which were not the crowns of rulers but rather crowns of victors, crowns awarded victors in the race. The implication is that these elders have already been rewarded, as is symbolized in the thrones.

In reconstructing the events of the end time, if the church is raptured before the end time events and is judged at the judgment seat of Christ, it would provide a plausible explanation that these twenty-four elders are representatives of the church.

John was then made aware of ominous sounds indicating divine judgment: "From the throne came flashes of lightning, rumblings and peals of thunder" (Rev. 4:5). The setting in heaven foreshadows the judgments to come on the earth. A similar experience of thunder, lightning, and trumpets was experienced in the giving of the Mosaic law in Exodus 19:16. The scene in heaven that John saw was, of course, the forerunner of the terrible judgments to be inflicted on the earth in the period that followed.

John then recorded, "Also in front of the throne there was what looked like a sea of glass, clear as crystal" (Rev. 4:6). Though the expression is not interpreted here, there seems to be a relationship to the laver or a bronze basin filled with water in the tabernacle in the Old Testament and the "Sea" in the temple (1 Kings 7:23–25), both of them being washstands designed to provide the priest with water for cleansing. Together they represent the sanctifying power of the Word of God symbolized by the water.

John continued, "In the center, around the throne, were four living creatures, and they were covered with eyes, in front and in back. The first living creature was like a lion, the second was like an ox, the third had a face like a man, the fourth was like a flying eagle. Each of the four living creatures had six wings and was covered with eyes all around, even under his wings" (Rev. 4:6–8). There is considerable diversity among interpreters concerning what the four living creatures represent. Probably the best interpretation is that they are physical embodiments of the attributes of God, as the seven lamps represent the Holy Spirit (v. 5). They are compared to a lion, an ox, a man, and a flying eagle. Some relate this to the four Gospels: Matthew represented the lion or the king; Mark, the ox or servant; Luke, man in his humanity; and John, the flying eagle representing the deity of Christ. Still others relate them to angels and find support in the fact that they had six wings. Their ministry was to worship God, and John recorded, "They do not rest day or night, saying: 'Holy, holy, holy, Lord God Almighty, who was and is and is to come'" (v. 8 NKJV).

Their worship of God also is a call to the twenty-four elders to worship. "Whenever the living creatures give glory, honor and thanks to him who sits on the throne and who lives for ever and ever, the twenty-four elders fall down before him who sits on the throne and worship him who lives for ever and ever" (vv. 9–10). The twenty-four elders also give their praise to the Lord, "They lay their crowns before the throne and say: 'You are worthy, our Lord and God, to receive glory and honor and power, for you created all things, and by your will they were created and have their being'" (vv. 10–11).

Though the entire content of chapter 4 is what John saw in heaven, it also is a revelation of the glory and honor given to God in the future and therefore has a prophetic base. Most important, it emphasizes what will occur in heaven while the end time events take place on earth.

THE WEDDING SUPPER ANNOUNCED

> Let us rejoice and be glad
>> and give him glory!
> For the wedding of the Lamb has come,
>> and his bride has made herself ready.
> Fine linen, bright and clean,
>> was given her to wear. (Rev. 19:7–8)

In Revelation 19:7–10, John was next introduced to the wedding of the Lamb, literally the marriage supper. This announcement has to be seen in the background of the ceremonies concerning marriage customs in the ancient world. When Christ was on earth, there were three major aspects to marriage tradition: First, parents of the bride and the bridegroom finalized the marriage contract, and the parents of the bridegroom would pay a dowry to the parents of the bride. This was the legal marriage process and the result would require a divorce to break the union. The second step, which usually occurred a year later or at another suitable time, featured the bridegroom accompanied by his male friends going to the house of the bride at midnight, then forming a torch parade through the streets. The bride would know he was coming and be ready with her maidens and would join the procession and go back to the home of the bridegroom. This is illustrated in the parable of the virgins in Matthew 25:1–13. The third phase of the wedding was a marriage supper that might go on for days as reflected in the wedding at Cana in John 2:1–12.

In view of this custom, it is significant that what is announced in Revelation 19 is the wedding feast, or supper, and the implication is that the first two steps of the wedding have taken place. This would fit naturally into the prophetic fulfillment of this illustration in that the legal phase of the wedding is consummated on earth when an individual believer puts his or her trust in Christ as Savior. The believer has been bought by the blood of Christ and now belongs to Christ in the sense of a betrothal. Accordingly, unfaithfulness for the bride in this situation is considered adultery.

The second phase of the marriage of the Lamb is illustrated in the rapture of the church when Christ comes to claim His bride and take her to the Father's house. The marriage supper of the Lamb would then follow as the third and final step.

As the narration of the events leading up to the second coming has been completed and the second coming itself is in view, it is significant that the wedding feast is now announced as if it were not consummated in heaven but is about to be consummated in connection with the second coming. Though many expositors believe that the wedding supper is in heaven, the evidence here at least suggests that the wedding feast could be connected with the second coming of Christ. It should be remembered that this will not be a literal feast with millions of people attending, but it is a symbolic concept in which the guests, or friends, of the bride and the bridegroom will join in the celebration of the marriage.

The bride is presented as being ready with fine linen bright and clean, which is defined as representing the righteous acts of the saints. Ephesians 5:25–27 speaks of the preparation of the bride: "Husbands, love your wives, just as Christ loved the church and gave himself up for her to make her holy, cleansing her by the washing with water through the word, and to present her to himself as a radiant church, without stain or wrinkle or any other blemish, but holy and blameless."

In preparation for the marriage, the Savior died on the cross for His church and became the sacrifice for her sin. This led to the present work of sanctification as the church is being cleansed during her period on earth with the washing of water through the Word, meaning the sanctifying truth of the Word of God is applied and in this way prepares the bride for her future role. The third and final state is at the rapture when the bride is presented in her perfection. There is no stain or discoloration, no wrinkle, no blemish, but in every respect the bride is holy and blameless. This, of course, is the result of the sanctifying work at the time of the rapture when the church is made like Christ.

Revelation 19:7–10 distinguishes those who are invited to the wedding feast and those who are not and also distinguishes the bride and those who are not the bride.

The figure of a marriage is used in the Old Testament of Israel, pictured as the unfaithful wife of Yahweh, whose spiritual restoration will take place in the future. The figure of marriage is also used of the church, where Christ is the bridegroom and the church is the bride. The wedding feast, to which the saints are invited, accordingly, includes the church as the bride of Christ and all others. This would include the Old Testament saints who are going to be raised at the second coming as well as the martyred dead of the tribulation who form the multitude. The fact that God deals differently with different people such as Israel, the church, and various nations is in keeping with His sovereignty. Actually, no two individuals are going through the world in exactly the same situation or have the exact same opportunities. God deals with each individual as well as each group on the basis of the qualities that are revealed in them.

NEW HEAVEN AND NEW EARTH

Having revealed the destruction of the old earth and the old heaven, John wrote that he saw what would take its place: a new heaven, a new earth, and a New Jerusalem (Rev. 21:1–8). "Then I saw 'a new heaven and a new earth,' for the first heaven and the first earth had passed away, and there was no longer any sea" (v. 1). Scriptural revelation gives very little information about the new earth, except by inferring that it is quite different from our present earth. The only major characteristic mentioned is that there will no longer be any sea in contrast to the present earth, which is mostly covered with water. It is apparent as the narration goes on that the new earth is round because there are directions of north, south, east, and west (v. 13), but there is no indication as to whether the new earth is larger or smaller than our present earth.

Instead of focusing on the new earth and a new heaven, Revelation deals with the subject of the Holy City, the New Jerusalem. John wrote, "I saw the Holy City, the new Jerusalem, coming down out of heaven from God, prepared as a bride beautifully dressed for her husband" (v. 2). The New Jerusalem is totally different from the old Jerusalem on the present earth and is created to be the center of population in the new earth.

Without explanation, John stated that the New Jerusalem comes down out of heaven from God. Though the new earth and new heaven are created at this time, apparently the New Jerusalem was created earlier. As the New Jerusalem will not be on the millennial earth, some have postulated the possibility that the New Jerusalem will be a satellite city over the earth during the millennium and as such would be the home of resurrected and translated saints. They would be able to go from New Jerusalem to the millennial earth much as people today have their homes in the countryside and go to work in the city. This would solve the problem of where the millions of resurrected and translated people live during the period when on earth there will be a population still living their natural lives, and no picture of the millennial earth takes into consideration the millions of those who are not in their natural bodies but who are serving the Lord. Because this has such a slender basis, however, it is a doctrine that cannot be held dogmatically.

The New Jerusalem is mentioned earlier in Scripture in a few passages (Isa. 65:17; 66:22; 2 Pet. 3:13; Rev. 3:12; 21:2). Several of these predictions of the New Jerusalem are found in contexts in which millennial truth is being discussed, and this has confused expositors as to how to relate the New Jerusalem to the millennial period. The answer is that in revealing future events, often events that are separated by time are merged as if they were in existence together. This is especially true, for instance, of the first and second comings of Christ, which in the Old Testament often are mentioned in the same verse (Isa. 61:1–2; see also Luke 4:17–19). In a similar way in Daniel 12:2, the resurrection of the righteous and the wicked are mentioned in the same verse, but later revelation reveals that there will be one thousand years between the resurrection of the righteous and the resurrection of the wicked. Malachi 4:5–6 alludes to the first and second comings of Christ. In the New Testament as well, similar events are put together that were separated by time as in 2 Peter 3:10–13, which refers to the beginning of the day of the Lord but then recounts events such as the destruction of heaven and the earth, which will take place at the end of the day of the Lord as well as the end of the millennium.

The absence of any sea in the new earth also makes it clear that this is not the millennium as some have tried to hold, for bodies of water are present in several millennial passages (Ps. 72:8; Isa. 11:9, 11; Ezek. 47:10, 15, 17–18, 20; 48:28). The tendency of some contemporary scholars to try to find fulfillment of the millennium in the new heaven and the new earth ignores these important differences in the description of the new earth as compared to the old earth. In the revelation to John of the new earth, new heaven, and New Jerusalem, it should be remembered that what John saw prophetically is what will happen in the future, not what existed at the time he lived on earth. John was projected forward in the history of the world to the time following the end of the millennium when this important change of scene will take place.

Some scholars also have been confused because the city is referred to as "prepared as a bride beautifully dressed for her husband" (Rev. 21:2). Some have tried to spiritualize the New Jerusalem as if it were a company of people. As Revelation continues, however, it is quite clear that it is a literal city that is intended, and the reference to it being beautiful like a bride refers to its newness. The setting of the New Jerusalem on the new earth is God's provision of a happy home for saints of all ages. Though not revealed in the Old Testament in any great length, Abraham, who looked for God's fulfillment in regard to the millennial kingdom, also looked for a heavenly city (Heb. 11:10–16; see also 12:22–24).

God will make His residence in the New Jerusalem; in fact, the New Jerusalem will be His temple. John wrote, "'He will wipe every tear from their eyes. There will be no more death' or mourning or crying or pain, for the old order of things has passed away" (Rev. 21:4). In making this statement, the revelation does not mean that we will start crying in heaven and then have our crying eased, but rather, it will be foreign to the whole setting. It will be a time of rejoicing in the grace of God and the opportunity and privilege of worship and service for the Lord. The situation will be an entirely new order, as John recorded, "He who was seated on the throne said, 'I am making everything new!' Then he said, 'Write this down, for these words are trustworthy and true'" (v. 5).

In a further summary of the character of heaven and of the New Jerusalem, John wrote:

> He said to me: "It is done. I am the Alpha and the
> Omega, the Beginning and the End. To the thirsty
> I will give water without cost from the spring of the
> water of life. Those who are victorious will inherit
> all this, and I will be their God and they will be
> my children. But the cowardly, the unbelieving,

the vile, the murderers, the sexually immoral, those
who practice magic arts, the idolaters and all liars—
they will be consigned to the fiery lake of burning
sulfur. This is the second death." (vv. 6–8)

In referring to Himself as "the Alpha and the Omega, the
Beginning and the End," Christ is saying that He is the first and the
last, as the first and last letters of the Greek alphabet are mentioned,
and this is further defined as the beginning and the end. Christ is the
eternal One, and the truths He is talking about are truths that will
last forever.

The wonder of salvation by grace and drinking of the spring of
the water of life are part of the wonderful provision God has made
for those who put their trust in Him. This refers to how abundant
our new life in Christ is as indicated in the invitation of Isaiah 55:1
and that of Christ in John 4:10, 13–14. The promise that all things
will be inherited by those who overcome by faith and that God will
be our God and we will be God's children is the illustration of the
abundant grace that Christians have in Christ and how marvelous
our inheritance is (Matt. 5:5; 19:29; 25:34; 1 Cor. 6:9–10; Heb.
1:14; 9:15; 1 Pet. 1:4; 3:9; 1 John 5:5).

Overcoming by faith is also mentioned as a ground for reward
in Christ's messages to the seven churches (Rev. 2–3) and is itemized as a hope and an expectation of Paul. "So then, no more
boasting about human leaders! All things are yours, whether Paul
or Apollos or Cephas or the world or life or death or the present
or the future—all are yours, and you are of Christ, and Christ is of
God" (1 Cor. 3:21–23).

Those whose lives are characterized by disregard of God and disregard of His moral commandments will be excluded. This revelation does not mean that if at one time in their lives some people were engaged in these immoral acts and thus cannot be saved; rather, it means if the quality of their lives as a whole is characterized by these sins, then their destiny will be the lake of fire. In Scripture, as in common life, sometimes people with sordid backgrounds are saved, forgiven, justified, and bound for heaven. Those who do not respond to faith in Christ have to face the fact that their destiny is the second death, the fiery lake of burning sulfur.

THE NEW JERUSALEM

Having surveyed the general character of the new earth and the New Jerusalem, John was then introduced to the Holy City, Jerusalem (Rev. 21:9–27). These verses near the end of the book of Revelation provide a vista for comprehending the beauty of the eternal situation in which Christians will find themselves when they are in the New Jerusalem and in the new earth.

One of the problems of interpretation is the question of how far nonliteral interpretation should figure in understanding Revelation 21:9–27. As a general rule, the basis for interpretation is best understood as providing a literal view of what is revealed but considering that the contents of what is seen may have spiritual meaning beyond the physical.

John wrote, "One of the seven angels who had the seven bowls full of the seven last plagues came and said to me, 'Come, I will show you the bride, the wife of the Lamb.' And he carried me away in the Spirit to a mountain great and high, and showed me the Holy City, Jerusalem, coming down out of heaven from God" (vv. 9–10). The problem mentioned in verse 2 of how a city could also be a bride carries over to this description. Actually, the bride of Christ comprises people who have accepted Christ in the present age and who form the church, the body of Christ. In showing John the Holy City, there is a relationship to the bride in that the beauty of the Holy City is similar to the beauty of the bride. Obviously, a literal meaning cannot be that it is both a city and a bride, and so one must complement the other.

John in his statement went on, "It shone with the glory of God, and its brilliance was like that of a very precious jewel, like a jasper, clear as crystal" (v. 11). Beginning with this verse, a number of precious jewels are mentioned as being characteristic of the New Jerusalem. Sometimes, however, it is difficult to ascertain exactly which jewel is in mind.

The city as a whole is like a precious jewel, "like a jasper, clear as crystal" (v. 11), according to John. In our present earth, the jasper stone is not clear but opaque, indicating that while the jewel looks like a jasper, it actually could be some other jewel. The description that follows pictures Jerusalem as a gigantic jewel piece aglow with the glory of God and a beautiful setting for God's grace to be made evident in the lives of those who have trusted Him.

The city as described by John is an impressive one even by present standards. Though some have said that the city is not a literal city and merely symbolizes the church, the body of Christ, it seems best to consider it a literal city that represents the church in some of its qualities. The wall of the city is described as great and high, which illustrates the fact that not everyone is qualified to enter into the blessings of the city. The number twelve is very prominent in the description of the city as seen in the twelve gates, the twelve angels, the twelve tribes of Israel (v. 12), the twelve foundations, the twelve apostles (v. 14), the twelve pearls (v. 21), and the twelve kinds of fruit (22:2). The city is also said to be twelve thousand stadia in length and the wall a hundred forty-four cubits thick, this number being twelve times twelve (21:16–17). The fact that the twelve gates have the names of the twelve tribes of Israel (v. 12) makes clear that Israel will be part of the populace of this city.

John, in his description of the city, continued, "There were three gates on the east, three on the north, three on the south and three on the west. The wall of the city had twelve foundations, and on them were the names of the twelve apostles of the Lamb" (vv. 13–14). Though the names of the twelve apostles are not given, it is clear that just as the names of Israel on the gates of the city prove that Israel is in the New Jerusalem, so the names of the apostles on the twelve foundations prove that the church will be in the New Jerusalem. As all the facts are put together, the New Jerusalem will be the home of all the saints of all ages and the holy angels as well as God Himself.

The immensity of this city is brought out by John's statement of the angel measuring the city. The twelve thousand stadia translated into modern terms amount to about fourteen hundred miles. The city as such would be far too large to place on the millennial earth, but on the new earth there will be plenty of room.

As stated, both Jew and Gentile will inhabit the city along with the saints of all other ages. Significant is the fact, however, that a Jew is not automatically recognized as belonging to the church and the church is not automatically related to Israel. The distinctions between the racial Jew and the church comprising both Jews and Gentiles are maintained in this revelation.

In Hebrews 12:22–24, the inhabitants of the city are itemized. "But you have come to Mount Zion and to the city of the living God, the heavenly Jerusalem, to an innumerable company of angels, to the general assembly and church of the firstborn who are registered in heaven, to God the Judge of all, to the spirits of just men made perfect, to Jesus the Mediator of the new covenant, and to the blood of sprinkling that speaks better things than that of Abel" (NKJV). In the New Jerusalem will be both angels and the church and all others who could be called righteous regardless of their dispensational background. Also in the city will be God the Father, God the Son, and God the Holy Spirit.

John described in detail the beautiful stones relating to the wall:

> The wall was made of jasper, and the city of pure gold, as pure as glass. The foundations of the city walls were decorated with every kind of precious stone. The first foundation was jasper, the second sapphire, the third agate, the fourth emerald, the fifth onyx, the sixth ruby, the seventh chrysolite, the eighth beryl, the ninth topaz, the tenth turquoise, the eleventh jacinth, and the twelfth amethyst. (Rev. 21:18–20)

These stones, having varied colors and glowing with the glory of God, presented an amazingly beautiful spectacle for John as he gazed on the city. The jasper stone, mentioned first, is apparently like our present jasper stone but clear as crystal. Built on the jasper stone, which is the bottom layer of the foundation, is a brilliant sapphire with the appearance of a diamond in color. The third foundation is an agate stone from Chalcedon, modern Turkey, and it is believed to have been sky blue with stripes of other colors. The fourth foundation, the emerald, introduces the familiar bright green color, and the onyx is a red and white stone. The sixth foundation, ruby, also identified as a sardius or carnelian stone, gives a reddish honey color. It is used with jasper in Revelation 4:3 describing the glory of God on the throne.

The seventh foundation is chrysolite, which is thought to have been a gold color, and possibly different from the modern chrysolite stone, which is a pale green. The eighth foundation, the beryl, is a deep sea green. The ninth foundation, the topaz, is yellow green, and transparent. The tenth foundation, turquoise, introduces another greenish color. The eleventh foundation, jacinth, is typically orange or violet in color. And the twelfth foundation, the amethyst, is commonly purple.

In seeing these many colors with the brilliant light of the glory of God in the New Jerusalem, John saw a scene of indescribable beauty worthy of the God who had created it. If Christians can be thrilled by the use of colors and the creations of men, how much greater will be the New Jerusalem, which comes from the creative hand of God.

John also referred to the twelve gates, "The twelve gates were twelve pearls: each individual gate was of one pearl" (Rev. 21:21 NKJV). Obviously these transcend any pearl such as we know in this life and are large stones, but they are beautiful like pearls. The streets to the city are declared to be of pure gold like transparent glass (v. 21). It is possible that all the materials of this city are translucent and the glory of God will go through them and light up the city in a blaze of color.

John next itemized things he did not see. "I did not see a temple in the city, because the Lord God Almighty and the Lamb are its temple" (v. 22). There apparently will be no sun or moon needed to bring light to the earth because the glory of God will light the New Jerusalem (v. 23). There will be no night either because the glory of God will illuminate the city continuously (v. 25). John stated, "The nations will walk by its light, and the kings of the earth will bring their splendor into it" (v. 24).

The nations, referring to the Gentiles, will bring their glory and honor into the city to the glory of God (v. 26). Anything that is impure, however, or is shameful or deceitful will be shut out of the city and not permitted to inhabit it, as John stated, "but only those whose names are written in the Lamb's book of life" (v. 27) will be allowed in the city. Though John's description is graphic and presents a beautiful display of the glory of God, it is obvious that the real city the believers will see in the eternal state will far exceed the possibility of describing it in words.

THE ETERNAL STATE

In the final chapter of the book of Revelation, the judgment of the wicked is viewed as past and eternity stretches before the believer. It is a time of unqualified blessing. John recorded, "Then the angel showed me the river of the water of life, as clear as crystal, flowing from the throne of God and of the Lamb" (Rev. 22:1).

In keeping with the holiness and perfection of the eternal state, the water of life flowed from the throne of God and of the Lamb. Scriptures mention other streams in the millennium, and this revelation should not be confused with the river that flows from the millennial sanctuary (Ezek. 47:1, 12), nor with the record of the living waters going forth from Jerusalem (Zech. 14:8). The water of life speaks of the purity, the power, and the holiness of the eternal life in the heavenly city. Significant is the fact that the water proceeds from the throne of God and of the Lamb. Though the throne of Christ is different from the throne of David and the millennial throne on which He sat throughout the millennial kingdom, this indicates that Christ is still with God the Father reigning over the eternal state.

In addition to picturing the water of life, John also noted the tree of life in the city. The water of life John described in Revelation 22:1 also is said to flow "down the middle of the great street of the city. On each side of the river stood the tree of life, bearing twelve crops of fruit, yielding its fruit every month. And the leaves of the tree are for the healing of the nations" (v. 2).

The question is asked fairly why healing would be necessary in a situation in which there is no sickness, no death, no sorrow, and no crime. Rather than healing, it could be understood as that which brings health. The leaves of the tree, then, would be described as bringing enjoyment of life in the New Jerusalem. Accordingly, as it may not be necessary to partake of the leaves of the tree in order to enjoy the eternal state forever, it apparently can enhance enjoyment. The healing is also said to extend to the nations, literally, the Gentiles or the peoples. Though frequently used to distinguish Gentiles from Israel, the word would include all races in a context such as this.

As if to answer the question of whether these verses imply imperfection in the eternal state, John stated, "No longer will there be any curse. The throne of God and of the Lamb will be in the city, and his servants will serve him" (v. 3). All that spoke of sin and its penalties is wiped away in heaven, and there is nothing left that is a reminder of sin. All are blessed, not cursed. In support of this conclusion, it is revealed that God's throne and that of the Lamb will be in the city. The question is often raised: What will Christians do in heaven? The Scriptures are very simple in stating the fact, as this verse does, that God's "servants will serve him" (v. 3). In a situation in which all children of God will be profoundly grateful for God's grace in bringing them to this place where they can enjoy the blessings of eternal life, the love of the saints for God will show itself in an eager desire to serve God. Whatever the humble task or the important task assigned to an individual, it will bring great satisfaction to be able to do something for God, who has done so much for that person.

The intimacy of the servants of God with God is indicated in that the saints will be able to see the face of God and His name will be on their foreheads. John wrote, "They will see his face, and his name will be on their foreheads" (v. 4). The identification with God is mentioned several times previously in the book of Revelation (2:17; 3:12; 7:3; 14:1). Seeing the face of God is something that could not have been accomplished prior to the saints' resurrection and glorification. The fact that they will be able to see the face of God demonstrates that they are perfectly holy by the grace of God.

Just as there will be a wonderful experience of relationship and service to God, so they will enjoy the glory of God. "There will be no more night. They will not need the light of a lamp or the light of the sun, for the Lord God will give them light. And they will reign for ever and ever" (22:5). Darkness will be banished in the eternal state. The New Jerusalem made of translucent materials will be an amazing, beautiful sight as the light streams through all the various colors, not leaving any shadows. The sun and the moon will be no more because they are no longer needed, and the glory of God will be the light of the city (21:23). The blessed state of God's servants is that they will reign with Christ forever.

As a climax to this revelation, John recorded, "The angel said to me, 'These words are trustworthy and true. The Lord, the God who inspires the prophets, sent his angel to show his servants the things that must soon take place'" (22:6).

An amazing record of God's faithfulness and sovereignty is demonstrated in history and climaxing in the eternal state. God has put down evil and judged Satan and people. No longer will people rebel against God, but God will be sovereign in time and eternity. No trace of sin will taint the kingdom of God, but the holiness that is God's own spiritual quality will be shared with the saints. Where once there was death, now there is resurrection life; where once there was judgment and curse, now there is removal and redemption; where once there was darkness, now there is light; where once there was ugliness, now there is beauty. Joy replaces sorrow; holiness replaces sin; and men and women, instead of serving themselves and Satan, will worship God, serve Christ, and be like Christ in spiritual quality.

Spiritually, there will be perfect restoration. In the conduct of government, there will be perfect administration. The servants shall be transformed into the likeness of God. They will clearly be identified with His name on their foreheads. No artificial means of light will be necessary because God will provide perfect illumination.

John was well aware, however, that the battle of the ages had not yet been consummated and that he still lived in the wicked world where he was in exile on the isle of Patmos. To him and to others caught still in the world's sinful state, the angel said, "Behold, I am coming quickly! Blessed is he who keeps the words of the prophecy of this book" (Rev. 22:7 NKJV). Though it is impossible to date the coming of Christ, the fact that the rapture of the church is an imminent event that requires preparation serves to alert believers that the events of the end time may be impending.

In Revelation 22:12–16, John recorded the repeated announcement of Christ's coming. In this final pronouncement by Jesus Himself, John was again reminded that Christ is coming like the morning star just before dawn and that when He comes it will be an abrupt event. It will be a time of judgment on the wicked and a time of reward for the saints. Christ again points out that He is Alpha and Omega, the first and last letters of the Greek alphabet; the First and the Last in terms of time; and the Beginning and the End in terms of creation (1:8, 17; 2:8; 21:6).

The final message of the book of Revelation is an invitation to partake of the water of life freely. "The Spirit and the bride say,

'Come!' And let the one who hears say, 'Come!' Let the one who is thirsty come; and let the one who wishes take the free gift of the water of life" (22:17).

Prophecy was written, on one hand, to warn sinners of God's judgment on them in the future with its appeal to come to God for the grace that He offers. By contrast also, prophecy describes for saints the blessings that will be theirs in eternity because they serve God in time. Readers of the book of Revelation who do not have the gift of eternal life are urged, accordingly, to accept the gift as God's free offer to be born again by faith in Christ and to be qualified to participate in what God has planned for those who love Him.

WHAT SHOULD
BELIEVERS DO NOW?

A cursory glance through the morning newspaper or evening television news will confirm that the world is in a state of turmoil. How will we know when Jesus's second coming is near? Scripture is full of parables and prophecies that point to clear indications that Jesus's earthly arrival is drawing close. Familiarizing ourselves with these passages can offer clarity and hope while also serving as a reminder of our role in a world of chaos.

LOOK FOR THE SIGNS

> Now learn this lesson from the fig tree: As soon
> as its twigs get tender and its leaves come out,
> you know that summer is near. Even so, when
> you see all these things, you know that it is near,
> right at the door. (Matt. 24:32–33)

Jesus first used the fig tree as an illustration of the signs of the Lord's coming (Matt. 24:32–33; Mark 13:28–29; Luke

21:29–31). A common interpretation has been to interpret the fig tree as a type of Israel and the revival of Israel as the budding of the fig tree. The fig tree could very well be a type of Israel, but it does not seem to be used as such in Scripture. Good and bad figs are mentioned in Jeremiah 24:1–8; the good figs are those carried off in captivity, and the bad figs remain in the land of Israel. Jeremiah 29:17 also talks about figs. In Judges 9:1–11, fig trees are mentioned but not in relation to Israel. Christ spoke about figs in Matthew 21:18–22 and Mark 11:12–14, 20–26, but no indication in the interpretation of those verses relates the fig tree to Israel. Accordingly, though many have followed this interpretation, there is no scriptural basis.

A better alternative is the simple explanation that the fig tree is used as a natural illustration. Because the fig tree by its nature brings forth leaves late in spring, seeing leaves on a fig tree is evidence that summer is near. This illustration is carried over to the second coming of Christ. When the events described in the preceding verses occur, it will be a clear indication of the second coming of Christ being near. The sign in the passage is not the revival of Israel, which is not the subject of Matthew 24, but rather the details of the great tribulation, which occurs in the three and a half years preceding the second coming. Accordingly, "all these things" (v. 33) refers not to the revival of Israel but to the events of the great tribulation. It is true, however, that Israel will have a measure of revival preceding the second coming of Christ, but this is based on other scriptural revelation rather than on the revelation presented here.

LIVE LIKE NOAH

> Therefore keep watch, because you do not know on
> what day your Lord will come. (Matt. 24:42)

Though the time of the coming of the Lord may be recognized as about to happen, details are not given in such clarity that one can determine the day or the hour. Needless speculation concerning the time of the coming of the Lord could be avoided if Matthew 24:36–42 were taken literally. Jesus said, "About that day or hour no one knows, not even the angels in heaven, nor the Son, but only the Father" (v. 36).

Jesus, of course, was referring here to His human intelligence, which was limited, not to His divine omniscience. The time leading up to the second coming was compared to the days leading up to the flood. In the case of the flood, there were numerous signs of the approaching end, and the same will be true of the second coming. It should be noted that the signs are in relation to the second coming of Christ at the end of the tribulation, not to the rapture of the church, which has no signs and is always imminent until it occurs. Noah took more than a hundred years to build the ark. In this time people carried on their normal activities, as Jesus mentioned (Matt. 24:37–38). When the ark was finally finished, however, the situation suddenly changed. Now it was possible for the flood to come.

As the flood neared, Noah's neighbors observed a very strange sight—animals marching into the ark in pairs, in almost military precision (Gen. 7:2–3). And God announced to Noah, "Seven days from now I will send rain on the earth for forty days and forty nights, and I will wipe from the face of the earth every living creature I have made" (v. 4).

After the animals had come safely into the ark, Noah and his family, consisting of his wife and three sons and their wives, also entered the ark. Now the situation was changed entirely. Everything that preceded the flood had now been fulfilled. The door to the ark was shut, and then it began to rain. In a similar way, many prophecies have to be fulfilled leading up to the second coming. As the period of the great tribulation progresses, and those who understand the prophecies of the end time realize that approximately three and a half years have passed, they will undoubtedly know and expect Christ to come even though the prophecies are not specifically detailed to allow them to know the day or the hour. Such people will know the year.

Jesus then compared the situation of the flood of Noah to the time of the second coming. He stated, "That is how it will be at the coming of the Son of Man. Two men will be in the field; one will be taken and the other left. Two women will be grinding with a hand mill; one will be taken and the other left. Therefore keep watch, because you do not know on what day your Lord will come" (Matt. 24:39–42).

Because this event is somewhat similar to the rapture in that some are taken and some are left, posttribulationists almost universally cite this verse as proof that the rapture will occur as a part of the second coming of Christ after the tribulation. However, a careful reading of the passage yields exactly the opposite result. At the rapture of the church, those taken are those who are saved, and those who are left are left to go through the awful period, including the great tribulation. Here the situation is in reverse. Those who are taken are taken in judgment, and those who are left are left to enter the millennial kingdom.

Despite the obvious fact that the illustration has to be reversed in order to make an application to the rapture, posttribulationists sometimes point out that the Greek word *airo*, used to express "took them all away" (v. 39), is a different word than used in verses 40 and 41 (*paralambano*: "will be taken"). Though admitting that in verse 39 at the time of the flood those taken were taken in judgment, posttribulationists claim the change in wording justifies reading the rapture into verses 40–42. However, this conclusion not only is contrary to the text of Matthew 24, but it also does not take into consideration Luke 17 in its description of the second coming, in which Jesus said, "I tell you, on that night two people will be in one bed; one will be taken and the other left. Two women will be grinding grain together; one will be taken and the other left" (vv. 34–35). In Luke, however, the question is asked by the disciples, "Where, Lord?" Jesus replied, "Where there is a dead body, there the vultures will gather" (v. 37). In other words, the ones taken are obviously put to death in judgment, in contrast to what will happen at the rapture when the ones taken are brought to heaven.

There is no scriptural basis for reading the rapture into Matthew 24. The occasion is entirely different. At the rapture, the church, comprising those who are saved, is taken to heaven. At the second coming of Christ, the saved remain on earth and the unsaved are taken away in judgment at the beginning of the millennial kingdom. The very word used to describe those taken away in Matthew

24:40–41 is used of Christ being taken away to the cross, obviously being taken in judgment as used here (John 19:16: "So the soldiers took charge of Jesus").

The conclusion for those living at the time of the second coming is similar to that of the time of Noah: "Therefore keep watch, because you do not know on what day your Lord will come" (Matt. 24:42). Though the passage is talking about the second coming of Christ and not the period preceding the rapture, if those living in the period before the second coming—who are able to see signs of the second coming indicating its approach—should be watching, how much more should those waiting for the rapture, which has no signs, live in constant expectation of the imminent return of Jesus for His church.

WATCH FOR THE OWNER OF THE HOUSE

Jesus made the application of watchfulness as would be required of the owner of a house who did not know when a thief would break in (Matt. 24:43). Not knowing the exact hour, he would have to watch continuously. Jesus applied this to those waiting for the second coming with the exhortation, "So you also must be ready, because the Son of Man will come at an hour when you do not expect him" (v. 44).

BE RESPONSIBLE STEWARDS

One who is waiting for the second coming of Christ is like a servant who is put in charge of his master's house. Not knowing when his master would return, the servant was urged to be faithful (Matt. 24:45–47). If, however, the servant takes advantage of his master and abuses his fellow servants and lives the life of a drunk-ard, he will experience the judgment of his master when the master returns unexpectedly (vv. 48–50). Jesus stated that the unfaithful servant will be cut in pieces and placed with the hypocrites (v. 51). The implication of this passage is that belief in the second coming of Christ is linked to belief in the first coming of Christ. If one accepts who Christ was and what He did in His first coming, he will also accept who Christ will be and what He will do at His second coming and, accordingly, will live in preparation.

BE PREPARED

As another illustration of the need for preparedness for the second com-ing, Christ described a familiar scene in Israel—that of the bridegroom claiming his bride (see Matt. 25:1–13). As noted before, the normal procedure was for a wedding to have three stages. First, the parents of the bridegroom would arrange for the marriage with the parents of the bride and would pay the dowry. This was the legal marriage. The second stage, which often took place a year or more later, was fulfilled when the bridegroom, accompanied by his friends, would proceed from the home of the bridegroom at midnight and go to the home of the bride and claim her. The bride would know that he was coming, would be ready with her maiden friends, and would join the procession from her home to the home of the bridegroom. The third phase of the traditional wedding was a marriage feast following this, which might take place for days and was illustrated in the wedding at Cana (John 2).

While the figure of bride and wife is used in more than one application in Scripture, normally, Israel is described as the wife of

the Lord, already married, and the church is pictured as a bride waiting for the coming of the Bridegroom (2 Cor. 11:2). At the rapture
of the church, the Bridegroom will claim His bride and take her to
heaven.

The illustration in Matthew 25 is in reference to the attendants
at the wedding. Each of the ten virgins took a lamp, but only the five
wise virgins took oil with their lamps. Though Scripture does not
explain the spiritual meaning of these elements, frequently in the
Bible the Holy Spirit is described as oil, as illustrated in the lamps
burning in the tabernacle and in the temple. When the cry rang out
that the bridegroom was coming (Matt. 25:6), the virgins all rose
to light their lamps and meet the procession. The foolish virgins,
however, had no oil at all, even in their lamps, and their wicks soon
burned out. When they requested oil from the wise virgins, they
were told to go buy some.

While they were out trying to make their purchase at midnight,
which could have been difficult, the five wise virgins went with the
procession to the home of the bridegroom, and Scripture recorded
that then the door was shut (v. 10). When the five foolish virgins
finally arrived, they were shut out because they were not watching for
the coming of the bridegroom and his procession.

As in all illustrations, the meaning of this one should not be
pressed to the point where it becomes a basis for doctrine. In this
case the main objective is clear. When the second coming occurs, it
is going to be too late to get ready. Though some have viewed this
incident as the rapture of the church, there is really no justification
for this because the context is entirely related to the second coming
of Christ, and Jesus had not yet revealed any truth concerning the

rapture. He could hardly, therefore, expect His disciples to understand an illustration of a truth that had not been revealed.

It is significant also that the bride is not mentioned—only the bridegroom. The ten virgins were not the bride but the attendants at the wedding, and this will apply, of course, to those who are waiting for the second coming of Christ. Though the interpretation relates to the second coming, there is an application of this truth to the rapture in the sense that preparedness for the rapture is just as necessary as preparedness for the second coming.

USE GOD'S GIFTS WELL

While Jesus was still in the vicinity of Jericho and on His way to Jerusalem, He used the parable of the ten minas to indicate the need for working while waiting for the return of the Lord (Luke 19:11–26). Luke recorded how the master gave his servants ten minas—one mina each to ten servants—and instructed them to invest their mina and use it to best advantage while he was gone to receive appointment as king. A mina was equivalent to three months' wages. Upon his return, one servant had gained ten minas and another five, and both were commended. However, the one who hid the mina and had not done anything with it was condemned by his master because he had not taken advantage of the opportunity of making this money work for his lord.

The account in Matthew of the parable of the talents has the same illustration, somewhat changed, which Jesus used in connection with His Olivet Discourse. In the parable of the talents, the master of the house gave to one five, another two, and another one talent and instructed the servants to work with this while he was gone. A talent was originally a weight of from fifty-eight to one hundred pounds. In modern value, a single silver talent is worth in excess of two thousand dollars, and a gold talent is worth in excess of thirty thousand dollars. In today's inflated prices, gold and silver are worth much more. In Jesus's time, a day's wages amounted to sixteen cents. Accordingly, these sums represented an enormous value.

In the illustration that Christ used, He was referring to silver talents as illustrated in the word *money* (Matt. 25:18), which is literally silver. In the illustration the master gave one servant five talents (or bags of gold, per NIV), another two, and another one, according to his estimate of their abilities. The master was gone for a long period of time, but when he returned, he called in his servants to give an account (v. 19). The five-talent man brought in an additional five talents, saying, "Master … you entrusted me with five bags of gold [talents]. See, I have gained five more" (v. 20). He was commended by his lord: "Well done, good and faithful servant! You have been faithful with a few things; I will put you in charge of many things. Come and share your master's happiness!" (v. 21). When the two-talent man reported, he, likewise, had doubled his money and received precisely the same commendation (vv. 22–23).

The one-talent man, however, had a different report: "'Master,' he said, 'I knew that you are a hard man, harvesting where you have not sown and gathering where you have not scattered seed. So I was afraid and went out and hid your gold [talent] in the ground. See, here is what belongs to you'" (vv. 24–25).

The master judged his servant, saying, "You wicked, lazy servant! So you knew that I harvest where I have not sown and gather where

I have not scattered seed? Well then, you should have put my money on deposit with the bankers, so that when I returned I would have received it back with interest" (vv. 26–27). The handling of the one-talent man is one of the major points of this illustration. Why was the master so hard on his servant? The answer is that the servant indicated he had serious questions as to whether the master would return. If the master did not, the servant could keep the money and not report it as part of his master's estate. If the master returned, he would be able to reproduce the talent and could not be accused of stealing. What the unprofitable servant displayed was lack of faith in his master and a desire to have his master's money illegally.

The point is that those who reject the truth of the return of the Lord are, in effect, nullifying the fact of His first coming, as acceptance of one should lead to acceptance of the other. In the illustration the master declared, "Take the bag of gold [talent] from him and give it to the one who has the ten bags [talents]. For whoever has will be given more, and they will have an abundance. Whoever does not have, even what they have will be taken from them. And throw that worthless servant outside, into the darkness, where there will be weeping and gnashing of teeth" (vv. 28–30).

As is brought out in 2 Peter 3:3–4, for one to question the literalness of Christ's second coming raises questions as to whether the person believed in the first coming. If Jesus is indeed the Son of God, then His coming again is both reasonable and to be expected. If He is not the Son of God, of course, He will not return. Accordingly, a lack of faith in the second coming stems from a lack of faith in the first coming. The one-talent man indicated outward profession of service to his master but did not possess real faith.

BE BLAMELESS

The extensive prophetic revelation, as well as Paul's counsel and exhortation to live for God, has its prophetic climax in the exhortation "May your whole spirit, soul and body be kept blameless at the coming of our Lord Jesus Christ" (1 Thess. 5:23). In referring to Christians as having spirit, soul, and body, Paul was recognizing the essential elements of human personality. Christians have a body, which will die but will be resurrected. They also have a soul, which refers to the psychological aspect of human life, and spirit, which seems to refer to their God consciousness and religious experiences. Though it can be demonstrated in Scripture that all these terms are sometimes used synonymously for an individual, and that the whole person is in view, nevertheless, these form the major constituent elements of human personality.

The reference to progressive sanctification obviously states that this is a work that only God can do. A believer in Christ can be part of the sanctification process by availing himself of the means to sanctification, such as the Word of God, prayer, fellowship with the Lord's people, and study of the Scriptures. In the end, however, God must do the sanctification, or it will not be effective. Paul anticipated the ultimate when all Christians will stand in heaven complete, with a new body, without sin, blemish, or defilement.

WAIT PATIENTLY FOR THE LORD'S COMING

A comparison is made between believers waiting for the coming of the Lord and the farmer waiting for his crop to mature. Just as the harvest is certain ahead, so the coming of Christ will climax our earthly work:

"Be patient, then, brothers and sisters, until the Lord's coming. See how the farmer waits for the land to yield its valuable crop, patiently waiting for the autumn and spring rains. You too, be patient and stand firm, because the Lord's coming is near" (James 5:7–8).

As James made clear, while we are waiting for the Lord's coming, we should be faithful in enduring suffering and be abundant in our service for the Lord. Especially, we should be engaged in prayer, recognizing that God hears and answers prayer (vv. 13–18).

BE CERTAIN OF OUR INHERITANCE

In keeping with the "living hope" given Christians "through the resurrection of Jesus Christ" (1 Pet. 1:3), they have a future inheritance that is being kept for them: "and into an inheritance that can never perish, spoil or fade ... kept in heaven for you" (v. 4). Meanwhile, as Christians are waiting for their inheritance, God protects them: "who through faith are shielded by God's power until the coming of the salvation that is ready to be revealed in the last time" (v. 5). This inheritance is certain because of God's promise in grace. Peter went on to say that persecutions and trials in Christ demonstrate the genuineness of a believer's faith.

FAITHFULLY ENDURE PERSECUTION

On the one hand, our inheritance is certain because of God's promise; on the other hand, it is certain because our faith is demonstrated through persecution: "These have come so that the proven genuineness of your faith—of greater worth than gold, which perishes even though refined by fire—may result in praise, glory and honor when Jesus Christ is revealed" (1 Pet. 1:7). Though persecutions for the time being prove difficult in any Christian's life, he may be encouraged by the fact that his faithfulness under these circumstances proves the genuineness of his faith and therefore his right to receive the reward that will be his in heaven. His persecutions will also be cause for praising Jesus Christ.

TRUST THAT THE WORD OF GOD REMAINS FOREVER

In contrast to that which is temporary, as illustrated in grass and flowers in the field, the statement was made, "the word of the Lord endures forever" (1 Pet. 1:25). The Christian may observe that our present world is decaying and will not endure forever. By contrast, the things that belong to our Christian faith will never cease to be true and will be supported by the Word of God, which stands forever.

BE CONFIDENT BEFORE THE LORD AT THE SECOND COMING

John warned his readers of apostasy and the importance of listening to the indwelling Holy Spirit as He distinguishes what is true and what is false. Consequently, the reader is encouraged to continue serving the Lord so that he will not be ashamed before Christ at His coming. "And now, dear children, continue in him, so that when he appears we may be confident and unashamed before him at his coming" (1 John 2:28). Though no Christian is able to lead a perfect life, the general tenor of his life serving the Lord or not serving the Lord will be evident at the time of divine judgment.

LOOK FORWARD TO BEING LIKE CHRIST

The previous exhortation to be serving Him when He comes is supported by the revelation of the love of the Father (1 John 3:1). John pointed out the importance of being called "children of God" (v. 2) now, even if we do not know what we will be. John stated, "Dear friends, now we are children of God, and what we will be has not yet been made known. But we know that when Christ appears, we shall be like him, for we shall see him as he is" (v. 2).

The fact that a believer will be able to see Christ at His appearing indicates that a transformation of believers in the world will take place. Several times in Scripture it is made clear that man in his natural state cannot endure being in the presence of the holy God. Paul, for instance, was stricken blind when he saw the glorified Christ (Acts 9:8), and the apostle John fell at the feet of Christ as though he were dead (Rev. 1:17). Accordingly, this scripture makes clear that when we see Him, we are going to be like Him. That is, that we will be without sin and will be able to stand comfortably in the presence of the holy God because Christ, when He appears, will appear to us and we will see His glory (Titus 2:13).

A further incentive is given to Christians to live for Christ now so that their lives will be without criticism when they stand in His presence. The application of this is found in the next verse of 1 John 3: "All who have this hope in him purify themselves, just as he is pure" (v. 3). This passage refers to the present work of sanctification, as "purify" is in the present tense. The whole doctrine of sanctification reveals that Christians should progressively become more and more like Christ in their lives on the earth, and they have the prospect of being perfectly like Him when they see Him.

The elements of sanctification are revealed in Scripture. The indwelling presence of the Holy Spirit is the Christian's guide and teacher. As Christians yield to Christ, they will experience the sanctifying power of the Word of God. The experience of prayer and fellowship with God is also a sanctifying experience. Mingling with other Christians who are serving God also constitutes a work of sanctification. Accordingly, the hope of Christ's appearing is an imminent event, which could occur at any time, and should spur a Christian to serve the Lord and continue in the process of sanctification in anticipation of the ultimate sanctification in Christ's presence.

ORDER OF EVENTS OF BIBLE PROPHECY

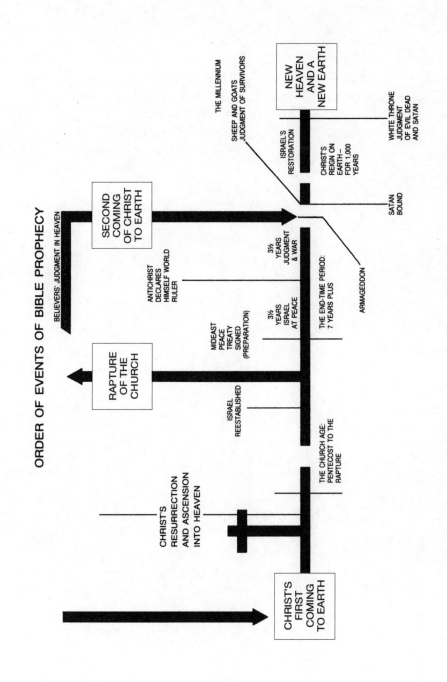

BELIEVERS' JUDGMENT IN HEAVEN

THE MILLENNIUM

SHEEP AND GOATS
JUDGMENT OF SURVIVORS

NEW HEAVEN AND A NEW EARTH

ISRAEL'S RESTORATION

WHITE THRONE
JUDGMENT OF EVIL DEAD
AND SATAN

SECOND COMING OF CHRIST TO EARTH

CHRIST'S REIGN ON EARTH—FOR 1,000 YEARS

SATAN BOUND

3½ YEARS
JUDGMENT & WAR

ANTICHRIST DECLARES HIMSELF WORLD RULER

THE END-TIME PERIOD:
7 YEARS PLUS

ARMAGEDDON

MIDEAST PEACE TREATY SIGNED (PREPARATION)

3½ YEARS
ISRAEL AT PEACE

RAPTURE OF THE CHURCH

ISRAEL REESTABLISHED

CHRIST'S RESURRECTION AND ASCENSION INTO HEAVEN

THE CHURCH AGE:
PENTECOST TO THE RAPTURE

CHRIST'S FIRST COMING TO EARTH

MAJOR EVENTS OF
UNFULFILLED PROPHECY

1. Rapture of the church (1 Cor. 15:51–58; 1 Thess. 4:13–18).
2. Revival of the Roman Empire; ten-nation confederacy formed (Dan. 7:7, 24; Rev. 13:1; 17:3, 12–13).
3. Rise of the Antichrist: the Middle East dictator (Dan. 7:8; Rev. 13:1–8).
4. The seven-year peace treaty with Israel: consummated seven years before the second coming of Christ (Dan. 9:27; Rev. 19:11–16).
5. Establishment of a world church (Rev. 17:1–15).
6. Russia springs a surprise attack on Israel four years before the second coming of Christ (Ezek. 38–39).
7. Peace treaty with Israel broken after three and a half years: beginning of world government, world economic system, world atheistic religion, final three and a half years before second coming of Christ (Dan. 7:23; Rev. 13:5–8, 15–17; 17:16–17).
8. Many Christians and Jews martyred who refused to worship world dictator (Rev. 7:9–17; 13:15).
9. Catastrophic divine judgments represented by seals, trumpets, and bowls poured out on the earth (Rev. 6–18).
10. World war breaks out focusing on the Middle East: Battle of Armageddon (Dan. 11:40–45; Rev. 9:13–21; 16:12–16).
11. Babylon destroyed (Rev. 18).

12. Second coming of Christ (Matt. 24:27–31; Rev. 19:11–21).

13. Judgment of wicked Jews and Gentiles (Ezek. 20:33–38; Matt. 25:31–46; Jude vv. 14–15; Rev. 19:15–21; 20:1–4).

14. Satan bound for one thousand years (Rev. 20:1–3).

15. Resurrection of tribulation saints and Old Testament saints (Dan. 12:2; Rev. 20:4).

16. Millennial kingdom begins (Rev. 20:5–6).

17. Final rebellion at the end of the millennium (Rev. 20:7–10).

18. Resurrection and final judgment of the wicked: great white throne judgment (Rev. 20:11–15).

19. Eternity begins: new heaven, new earth, New Jerusalem (Rev. 21:1–2).

PREDICTED EVENTS RELATED
TO THE NATIONS

1. United Nations organized as first step toward world government in 1945.
2. Israel is formed as a recognized nation in 1948.
3. Europe is rebuilt after World War II, setting stage for its role in the future revival of the Roman Empire.
4. The rise of Russia as a world military and political power.
5. World movements such as the European Union and the World Bank set the stage for future political and financial events.
6. China becomes a military power.
7. The Middle East and the nation of Israel become the focus of worldwide tension.
8. The Arab oil embargo in 1973 results in world recognition of the power of wealth and energy in the Middle East.
9. Lack of a powerful political leader prevents the Middle East from organizing as a political power.
10. The rapture of the church removes a major deterrent to expansion of political and financial power of the Mediterranean world.
11. A new leader arises in the Middle East; this leader is later identified as the Antichrist, who secures power over first three, and then all ten nations, uniting them in a Mediterranean confederacy.

12. The new Mediterranean leader imposes a peace settlement for seven years on Israel.

13. Russian army, accompanied by several nations, invades Israel and is destroyed by judgments from God.

14. Peace settlement in the Middle East is broken after three and a half years.

15. Middle East ruler becomes a world dictator as the Antichrist.

16. Middle East ruler claims to be God and demands that all worship him at pain of death.

17. Middle East dictator defiles the temple in Jerusalem.

18. The terrible judgments of the great tribulation—described in the seals, trumpets, and bowls of the wrath of God in the book of Revelation—begin.

19. There is worldwide discontent at the rule of the Middle East ruler, resulting from many catastrophes and causing rebellion and gathering of the world's armies in the Middle East to fight it out, with Armageddon as the center of the conflict.

20. Second coming of Christ occurs; Christ is accompanied by the armies from heaven.

21. The armies of the world attempt to fight the armies from heaven but are totally destroyed.

22. Christ's millennial reign is established, climaxing judgments on all the unsaved and the final disposition of Gentile political power.

23. Those saved (both Jews and Gentiles) are placed in the New Jerusalem on the new earth where they will spend eternity.

PREDICTED EVENTS RELATED
TO THE CHURCH

1. Rise of liberalism and rejection of fundamental biblical doctrines permeate the professing church.
2. Communism and atheism rise as major opponents of Christianity.
3. The ecumenical movement promoting a world church organized in 1948.
4. Increased moral chaos results from departure from biblical doctrines.
5. Evidence of spiritism, the occult, and Satan worship increases.
6. The church is raptured.
7. The Holy Spirit lifts the restraint of sin.
8. "Super church" movement gains power and forms a world church.
9. World church works with the Antichrist to secure world domination.
10. Super church is destroyed by the ten leaders supporting the Antichrist to pave the way for worship of the world ruler as God.
11. Those who have come to believe in Christ as Savior since the rapture suffer persecution because they refuse to worship the world ruler.
12. Second coming of Christ occurs, and remaining Christians in the world are rescued and enter the millennial kingdom.
13. After the millennium the church is placed in the New Jerusalem on the new earth.

PREDICTED ORDER OF PROPHETIC EVENTS RELATED TO ISRAEL

1. The holocaust and suffering of Jews in World War II lead to worldwide sympathy for the Jews, resulting in their transition to a homeland.

2. In 1948, the United Nations recognizes Israel as a nation and allows her to have five thousand square miles of territory, excluding ancient Jerusalem.

3. Israel, though immediately attacked by those nations surrounding her, achieves increases in territory in subsequent wars.

4. Though Russia at the beginning is sympathetic to Israel, the United States becomes her principal benefactor and supplier of military aid and money.

5. Israel makes amazing strides forward in reestablishing her land and its agriculture, industries, and political power.

6. In a series of military tests, Israel establishes that her army is superior to those of surrounding nations.

7. Arab power opposing Israel is sufficient to keep Israel from having peaceful coexistence with other nations in the Middle East.

8. Israel continues in a state of confusion and conflict until the church is raptured.

9. With the formation of the ten-nation confederacy by a Gentile ruler in the Middle East, Israel is forced to accept a seven-year peace settlement.

10. The world and the Jewish people celebrate what appears to be a permanent peace settlement in the Middle East.

11. Israel prospers, and many return to Israel after the peace is settled.

12. Toward the close of the three and a half years of peace, Russia, accompanied by several other nations, attempts to invade Israel but is destroyed by a series of judgments from God.

13. After three and a half years of peace, the covenant is broken, and the Middle East ruler becomes a world dictator and a principal persecutor of Israel.

14. The world dictator desecrates the temple of Israel and sets up an idol of himself to be worshipped.

15. Worldwide persecution of the Jews begins, and in the land two out of three perish.

16. A Jewish remnant who puts trust in Christ emerges.

17. Though the world ruler massacres both Jews and Gentiles who fail to worship him as God, some survive and are rescued by Christ.

18. The second coming of Christ rescues persecuted Jews and Gentiles and brings judgment on all wickedness in the world and unbelievers.

19. The promised kingdom on earth—with Jesus as Israel's Messiah and David as her regent prince—begins with godly Israel being regathered from all over the world to inhabit her Promised Land.

20. For one thousand years Israel experiences unusual blessing as the object of Christ's favor.

21. With the end of the millennial kingdom and the destruction of the present earth, godly Israel has its place in the eternal state and the new heaven and the new earth.

22. Those among Israel who are saved are placed in the New Jerusalem on the new earth.

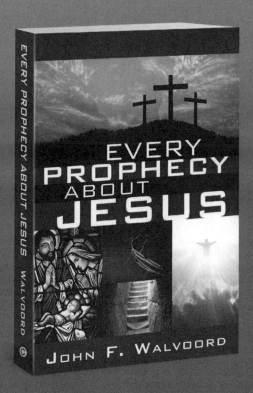

A Faith-Building Guide to Biblical Prophecies about Christ

We believe that Jesus Christ saved us from our sins. But what can we learn about Jesus—and our own relationship with God— through the Bible's prophecies about Him? This comprehensive guide shows the remarkable accuracy of biblical predictions about Christ and why they matter to us today.

David C Cook

transforming lives together